THE ENCYCLOPEDIA OF
KNITTING
& CROCHET
for
BLOCKS, BLANKETS
& THROWS

THE ENCYCLOPEDIA OF
KNITTING
& CROCHET
for
BLOCKS, BLANKETS
& THROWS

LUISE ROBERTS

Search Press

A QUARTO BOOK

Published in 2008 by Search Press Ltd
Wellwood
North Farm Road
Tunbridge Wells
Kent TN2 3DR

ISBN 978-1-84448-322-8

Conceived, designed and produced by
Quarto Publishing plc
The Old Brewery
6 Blundell Street
London N7 9BH

QUAR.EMAT

Senior Editor Liz Dalby
Copy Editor Diana Chambers
Additional text and images (pages 58 to 67) Betty Barnden
Pattern Checker Carol Chambers

Art Director Caroline Guest
Managing Art Editor Anna Plucinska
Art Editor Julie Francis
Photographer Martin Norris
Picture Research Claudia Tate

Creative Director Moira Clinch
Publisher Paul Carslake

I would like to dedicate this book to my mother, Margaret Roberts, who has taught me more than will ever be found in books.

CONTENTS

FOREWORD

What drew me to blankets and throws was very much a need: the need for small, portable projects; for baby blankets, chair throws for old secondhand chairs and the need to make a new house a home. There is nothing more comforting than a throw wrapped around your shoulders against the chill of summer evenings and there's nothing more loving than giving this pleasure to my daughter.

At first it seemed there might be a problem. I don't like repeating myself too often, but at the same time I do like easy visual rhythms and simple design. This set me off on a quest to see just how many different shapes I could create and what solutions there were to the inevitable problem of the wrong side facing out, and to thinking about the blanket as a garment and about fit and drape. It is far more than just a flat piece of knitting; lace is revealing, texture may need taming and edging and trimming possibilities are infinite.

If you fall solely into either the knit or crochet camp I hope you may come to appreciate the benefits of the other and perhaps learn a technique or two. Making a blanket or throw is a big enough project without any prejudices about techniques that can help you to achieve a better finish with less stress.

ABOUT THIS BOOK

THE BASICS (pages 8–19)

An illustrated guide to choosing the best tools and materials for the project in hand, including rules of thumb for substituting yarns and calculating the right number of yards for blankets small or large, knitted or crocheted.

DESIGNING BLANKETS AND THROWS (pages 20–97)

The creative fun starts here! Full instructions and stitch patterns are supplied for how to incorporate two or more colours in a piece; creating simple stripes or working complex colourwork patterns; incorporating texture using beads, bobbles, lace or woven samples; and adding decorative edges and plain or fancy seams.

STITCH DIRECTORY (pages 98–119)

A collection of exciting stitch patterns and motifs for knit and crochet. Samples are coded by skill level so beginners can choose easy stitch patterns and more experienced knitters and crocheters can select more challenging ones.

PROJECTS (pages 120–133)

A collection of charming projects to try out your skills, from a Fair Isle throw in rich autumn shades to a delicate cashmere bed throw in filet crochet.

RESOURCES (pages 134–139)

Useful information on abbreviations and symbols used throughout the patterns; hook and needle sizes and yarns used in the samples.

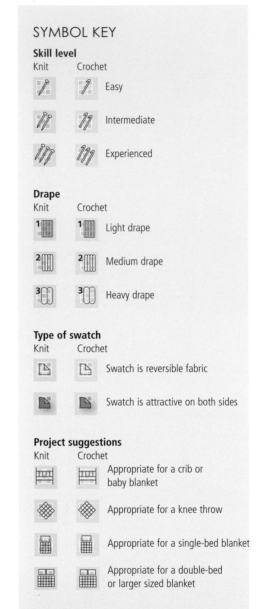

SYMBOL KEY

Skill level

Knit	Crochet	
		Easy
		Intermediate
		Experienced

Drape

Knit	Crochet	
1	1	Light drape
2	2	Medium drape
3	3	Heavy drape

Type of swatch

Knit	Crochet	
		Swatch is reversible fabric
		Swatch is attractive on both sides

Project suggestions

Knit	Crochet	
		Appropriate for a crib or baby blanket
		Appropriate for a knee throw
		Appropriate for a single-bed blanket
		Appropriate for a double-bed or larger sized blanket

Colour coding

Throughout, colour coding distinguishes between crochet and knitted samples: blue is for knitting; cream is for crochet.

DESIGNING BLANKETS AND THROWS

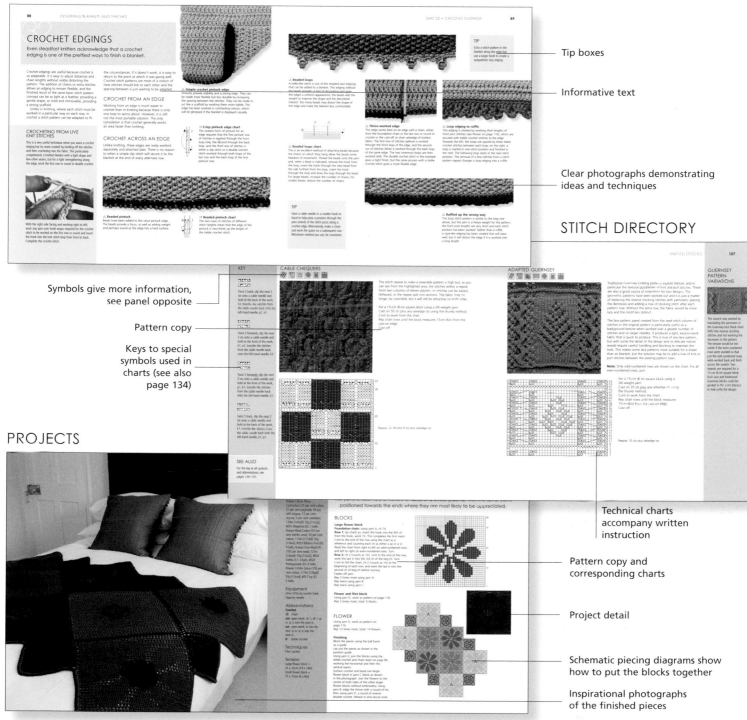

Tip boxes

Informative text

Clear photographs demonstrating ideas and techniques

STITCH DIRECTORY

Symbols give more information, see panel opposite

Pattern copy

Keys to special symbols used in charts (see also page 134)

PROJECTS

Technical charts accompany written instruction

Pattern copy and corresponding charts

Project detail

Schematic piecing diagrams show how to put the blocks together

Inspirational photographs of the finished pieces

TOOLS FOR KNITTING AND CROCHET

The range of equipment and materials for making blankets and throws is enormous, and the success of your project may rest on the choices you make.

It is possible to spend years looking for the perfect tool, but very often practice and an improved technique are all that is required. For almost every other craft, there is a right way and wrong way of doing things, but in knitting and crochet there is just what is comfortable and pleasing.

A range of basic equipment will probably suffice for most of your needs, but there is always room to delight in the pretty stitch markers and the hand-crafted beech knitting needles or crochet hooks that are available.

Needles and hooks are perhaps the most important equipment that you need

to invest in, and are available in a range of materials and sizes. The yarn and the drape of the fabric will determine which needle or hook size you will need; every pattern starts with a suggested tension and size to obtain that tension. Most of the sizes can be found in a range of materials, although smaller needles and hooks are usually made in rigid metal, while the larger ones are made in bamboo, or hollow metal and plastic. It's a matter of personal choice which you prefer to work with.

METAL TOOLS

Aluminium is slippery and allows for faster knitting or crocheting and, in the case of knitting, ease of stitch transfer. Metal knitting needles often have longer and more tapered points, which are excellent for lace knitting. Metal can also be found in a variety of colours, especially if vintage equipment is sought, but the shine reduces the potential colour contrast with the yarn.

RESIN AND PLASTIC TOOLS

Resin and plastic needles and hooks are warmer to use and more flexible than metal needles and hooks, and although they are also smooth, the stitches or stitch wraps are less likely to slide about. The moulding process allows for points of a variety of shapes and they can vary greatly from fairly tapered to quite blunt and round. The very blunt, rounded points are slightly harder to work with, but are very useful when working with thick or loosely spun yarn. Resin and plastic needles and hooks can be found in a variety of wonderful colours that are a delight, as well as providing a useful contrast to the yarn of the project.

WOOD AND BAMBOO TOOLS

Wood and bamboo make the lightest tools with the greatest flexibility, and they improve with age. The extra friction they provide makes them perfect for stitch patterns with a lot of yarnovers or wraps of yarns that tend to slip. The points can be gently sanded to suit individual needs.

YARN HOLDER

This solution to the age-old problem of working and walking is a recent discovery inspired by a project by Meta Thompson in the Interweave magazine *Spin Off*. It is useful if the weather is too warm for garments with pockets, and this bag is large enough that the yarn can flow more smoothly than when in a pocket. Make it by piecing any two 15-cm (6-in) lacy blocks together and adding an 20-cm (8-in) strap for a handle. It is designed to hang from the wrist of the hand in which you hold the yarn. (For this block pattern see page 118.)

Use the spokes to represent the position of numbers on a clock face and keep track of the last row of a repeat worked by moving a stitch marker to the appropriate number position on the bag.

For work involving more than one length of yarn, pass the yarns through different sections of the same fascia to help prevent the yarns from tangling.

Keep safety pins and cable needles handy by pinning them to the fabric.

1 Knitting needles

Needles are available in three types: straight, double-pointed and circular. For working on blocks, short straight needles or circular needles are ideal. For large knit-in-one piece blankets and throws, long circular needles are essential. For long, picked-up edgings, the longest circular needles are very useful; you could use a series of long double-pointed needles, but you run the risk of dropping stitches.

2 Crochet hooks

Crochet hooks vary in size, the material they are made of and the style of the handle. Hooks with a larger, flatter, handle tend to be easier to manoeuvre and require a less firm handgrip. The depth and width of the hook and the width of the "throat" vary, and greatly influence the shape of the stitch. Keep a crochet hook in your knitting bag for picking up stitches.

3 Cable needles

Cable needles hold stitches out of the way while cables and crosses are worked. They may be straight, or have a V-shaped kink in them that helps prevent the stitches sliding off accidentally.

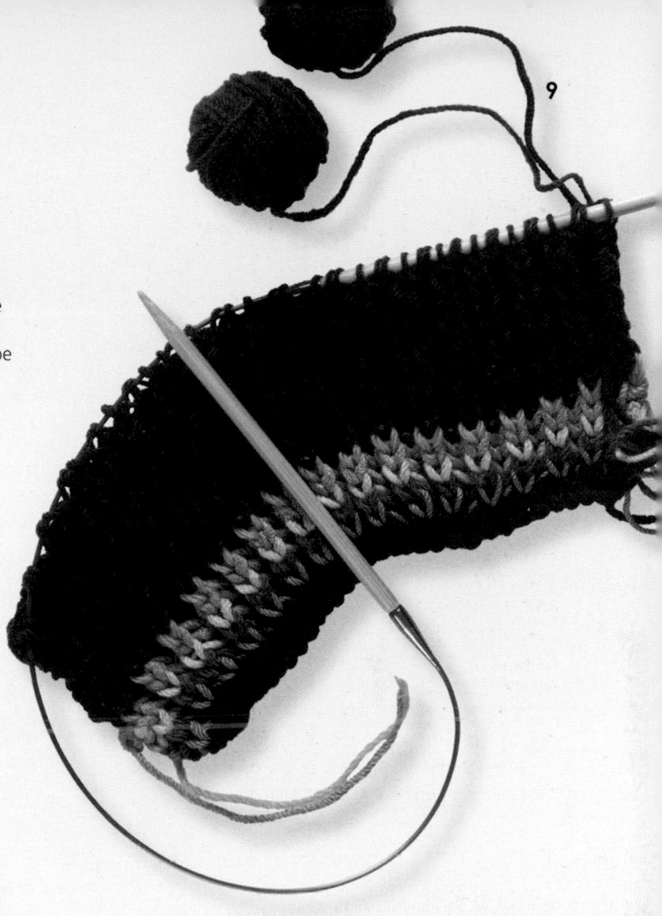

▷ Circular needles

These are useful not only for working on all-in-one blankets but also for working on smaller projects when you are out and about. They are more discreet than straight needles, and there is no risk of one needle dropping to the floor.

9

1

Aluminium needles

Plastic needles

Bamboo needles

Bamboo needles with row counter

Double-pointed wooden needles

2

Aluminium crochet hook

Wooden crochet hook

Plastic crochet hooks

3

Cable needles

4 Point protectors

Point protectors protect the needle tips and the workbag from damage, and can help keep stitches secure when you are not working on a project.

5 Bobbins

Bobbins are ideal for holding lengths of yarn when you are working blocks or short repeats of colour. They allow the controlled release of yarn, helping to prevent it from tangling.

6 Stitch marker

Stitch markers are invaluable for marking the start and end of repeats and the position of decreases. They help to establish a rhythm that will prompt what comes next or indicate an error on the previous row. Loops of waste yarn work well; or try beaded earring loops or small safety pins.

7 Split-ring stitch marker

Split-ring stitch markers or earring hooks can be used to mark a place in a worked fabric. They are especially useful in crochet where they can be looped through the top of a worked stitch. Take care to avoid distorting the fabric.

8 Row counter

A row counter is particularly useful if you are working on a project in short bursts.

9 Tape measure

For measuring long lengths, a tape measure is invaluable. Choose a fibreglass measure with both imperial and metric scales.

10 Small ruler

A small ruler is excellent for measuring small blocks and can also be placed along the base of a row to check the stitches along it.

11 Scissors

A pair of small pointed scissors – preferably in a sheath or case to protect your workbag – is essential. (Avoid breaking yarn as this will stretch the fibres, is less predictable than cutting and will make threading a needle more difficult.)

12 Wooden ruler

A solid ruler for blocking and measuring longer edges is useful for finishing a blanket.

13 Safety pins

Small safety pins are ideal for seaming. They don't slide out when holding pieces together, and allow selvedges to be positioned together edge-to-edge.

14 Pins

You should have a supply of pins in a range of lengths – longer ones for quick marking out and pinning; shorter ones for blocking.

15 Tapestry needles

Blunt-tipped tapestry needles are essential for weaving in ends. Use a size appropriate for your yarn. A larger size may be easier to thread, but it will be more difficult to weave the end in and this may distort the fabric.

16 Sewing needle and thread

A needle and thread are useful for threading beads onto yarn and for marking stitches or rows.

17 Length of wire

Use a length of wire folded in two to thread beads onto yarn. Grip the yarn in the bend and push the two ends of the wire through the bead, which then passes down the wire and onto the yarn.

18 Small notebook and pen

Record your project's progress in a notebook – inspiration or motivation, yarns (shades and batch numbers) and needles or hooks used. Tick off what you have done, and note any new ideas to try or complicated pattern instructions.

BEADED STITCH MARKERS

Making your own stitch markers doesn't take long and requires no special equipment. The weight of the beads makes them quicker and easier to transfer from one needle to the next than plastic stitch markers.

Gather some 1.2-cm (½-in) split rings, some 5-cm (2-in) eye pins and a selection of small and large beads no bigger than 1.2cm (½in) across. Beads may be simple or decorative like the glass fish bead, below.

Thread beads onto eye pins to a depth of about 2.5–3.8cm (1½in). Secure them by using a pair of round-nosed pliers to grip the end of the eye pin and twist the wire around the pliers to make a loop.

Open the split ring by moving one end to the side slightly. Do not pull the ends apart in opposite directions, as this will distort the ring. Thread on the eye pin with the beads and slide the ends of the split ring together again. Making your own stitch markers in this way will enable you to develop your own colour coding system. As well as split rings you can use ear wires, as shown here.

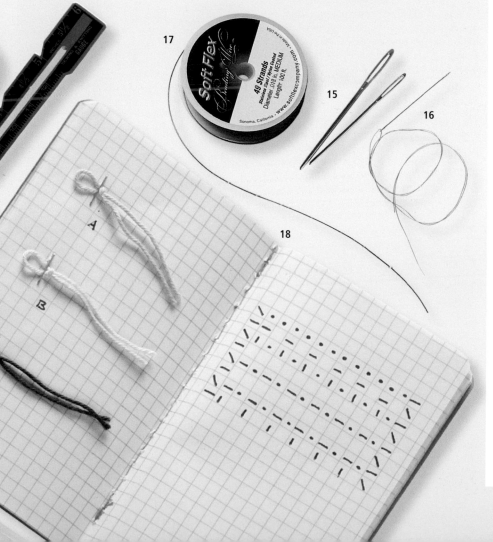

17

15

16

18

2 YARN

Yarn can be created from any animal, vegetable or mineral fibre that can be spun into a continuous, flexible and durable length. The imagination and skill of spinners results in a huge array of yarns.

Cotton

The first thing to consider is the weight of the yarn, which for a blanket depends very much on the style of the project. The yarn weight is determined by the number of plies, the yarn thickness and the air held within it. This may be very hard to judge without seeing or working the yarn as similar-sounding yarns can vary from spinner to spinner. In the US, the Craft Yarn Council of America has compiled a useful table (below), which magazines and books are using increasingly to specify their yarns.

The next important decision concerns the type of fibre. It may be that the choice of yarn prompted you to make a blanket, in which case it is a matter of making swatches of some possible designs and deciding which works best. Otherwise, if you have a pattern in mind, you will need to choose between natural fibres, synthetics or a mixture.

SYNTHETICS

Acrylic, polyester and nylon are made from oil and are soft, hardwearing and machine-washable – ideal for baby blankets or throws that will be roughly handled. However, it can be difficult to get an even finished fabric; synthetics have little stretch and don't respond well to blocking – what you knit is what you get.

NATURAL FIBRES

These can be split into animal fibres – wool, cashmere, angora, alpaca and silk – and vegetable fibres – cotton, linen, bamboo and soy. Rayon and viscose are vegetable fibres but have been processed to have similar properties to synthetics. In general, natural fibres are warm when it is cold and cool when it is hot. They tend to improve with blocking, drape better and last longer than synthetics.

MIXES AND NOVELTY YARNS

Fibre mixes often combine the versatility and warmth of natural fibres with the practicality of synthetics – cashmere and wool, or wool and cotton, for example. There is also a huge range of novelty yarns with unusual textures. Examples include felted, slub, chenille, bouclé, fur, mohair, ladder, ribbon and Lurex. These can add a glamorous touch to a blanket project, but working a swatch and washing it several times is essential before deciding whether or not they will stand the test of time.

Yarn specifications

Type of yarns in category	Sock, fingering, baby	Sport, baby	DK, light worsted	Worsted, afghan, aran	Chunky, craft, rug	Bulky, roving
Knit tension ranges in stockinette stitch to 10cm (4in)	27–32 sts	23–26 sts	21–24 sts	16–20 sts	12–15 sts	6–11 sts
Recommended needle in metric size range	2.25–3.25mm	3.25–3.75mm	3.75–4.5mm	4.5–5.5mm	5.5–8mm	8mm and larger
Recommended needle US size range	1 to 3	3 to 5	5 to 7	7 to 9	9 to 11	11 and larger
Crochet tension ranges in single crochet to 10cm (4in)	21–32 sts	16–20 sts	12–17 sts	11–14 sts	8–11 sts	5–9 sts
Recommended hook in metric size range	2.25–3.5mm	3.5–4.5mm	4.5–5.5mm	5.5–6.5mm	6.5–9mm	9mm and larger
Recommended hook US size range	B–1 to E–4	E–4 to 7	7 to I–9	I–9 to K–10½	K–10½ to M–13	M–13 and larger

▷ Ball band information

You can find the technical information about a ball of yarn on the ball band, as shown here. Working a swatch with the yarn and washing it will reveal its true nature.

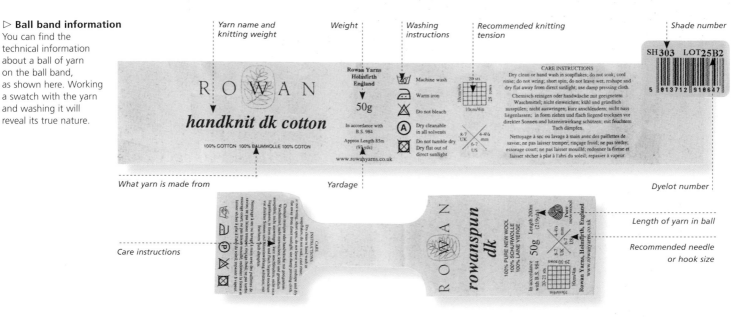

Yarn name and knitting weight

Weight

Washing instructions

Recommended knitting tension

Shade number

What yarn is made from

Yardage

Dyelot number

Care instructions

Length of yarn in ball

Recommended needle or hook size

WOOL

Wool is spun from sheep's fleece and is warm, flexible, hardwearing, easy to work and always looks good. There are as many different types of wool as there are different breeds of sheep.

CASHMERE

Made from the coat of a cashmere goat, cashmere yarn is particularly light, soft, warm and easy to use, but tends to be expensive.

ALPACA

Alpaca yarn is made from alpaca's hair (similar to a llama) and is fine, soft, warm and relatively inexpensive.

Wool

ANGORA

Made from the hair of an Angora rabbit, this yarn is warm and light but often quite fluffy, so does not show texture or lace patterns at their best.

SILK

Silk is a luxury yarn made by the larvae of silkworms. It has a beautiful drape and feel, but isn't durable, and is very expensive. Silk is not suitable for a blanket project unless it is mixed with another fibre.

COTTON

Produced from the seed head of the cotton plant, this fibre is hardwearing and smooth, but non-elastic. It is heavy and will stretch if hung, although washing can restore its shape. Mercerized cotton has been treated to give it shine and strength. Cotton shows texture off well, but dense stitching will make the fabric even heavier.

BAMBOO AND LINEN

Made from the plant fibres of bamboo and hemp respectively, these yarns have very similar properties to cotton.

SOY

Soy yarn is spun from the by-product of tofu production. The fibres are environmentally friendly, light and warm.

CARING FOR YOUR BLANKET

A blanket or throw will have taken a considerable investment of your time and money. Washing it gently and rolling dry in some towels on a flat surface will prolong its life. Of course, synthetic yarns can tolerate rougher treatment and the ball band will always give a washing guide, but if the blanket contains a mix of yarns, then always launder according to the directions for the most delicate yarn. To ward off moths, never store a blanket if it is dirty. Fold it in a pillow case to keep the dust off or wrap a towel around it, and store in a cupboard, preferably with some cedar balls. If you do discover moths, check everything made from wool, including stored yarn, and wash anything that looks or feels as if it may be affected by them.

3
THE PERFECT FIT

Always start a project knowing the tension of the fabric.
If you don't you will not know the finished size, the
amount of yarn required or indeed how the finished
project will drape.

The tension of a fabric is described by the
number of stitches and rows over a given
distance, usually 10cm (4in). In order to
calculate the tension of a fabric, a tension
swatch is worked. The starting point for this
can be, in order of importance: the tension
mentioned in the pattern, the tension suggested
on the ball band, or the suggested tension
given in the table on page 12.

▽ **Checking your tension**
Count stitches and rows against a wooden
ruler or a solid straight edge. It is easier to
see and count the stitch fractions at the
end of the measure. A spare knitting
needle or crochet hook makes a
useful pointer to count off the
stitches and rows.

WORKING A SWATCH

Start working a tension swatch by using the
suggested needle or hook size and casting on
or working a foundation chain with half again
more stitches than the stated tension for
10cm (4in). Work the pattern stated for
15cm (6in) and bind or fasten off the yarn.
Then pin the swatch onto a firm surface such
as a blocking board, ironing board or firm
cushion, and block it as suggested in the
pattern (see page 78). Remove the pins and
lay the work on a flat surface. Using pins as
markers, pin out an area in the middle of the
swatch 10cm (4in) square and count horizontally
along the row the number of stitches, and
vertically the number of rows, that fall
within this area.

*A piece of cardboard with a
10-cm (4-in) square cut in
it is a useful addition to the
workbag. It can be used
to count stitches or rounds
within a 10-cm (4-in)
square area.*

STITCH COUNT

If the number of stitches is too few, then
the stitches are too big and another tension
swatch is needed, but worked using smaller
needles or hook. If the number of stitches is
too many, then the stitches are too small and
another tension swatch is needed, but this time
worked using larger needles or hook.

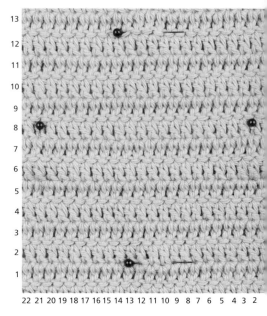

△ **Tension swatch**
For small adjustments in the tension try using
the same size hook but with a different hook
or handle shape. The way the hook is used
will change the stitches slightly.

TIP

Store and wash the
tension swatches with
the finished blanket.
They may be useful for
making repairs at a
future date.

ROW COUNT

If the stitch count is correct but the row count is not, try working either more or fewer rows. In crochet, if the row count is slightly low, this can be adjusted by working one more chain in the row start chains. In knitting, if the stitch count is correct but the row count is not, you can solve this problem by working more or less rows. Alternatively, you can work with two slightly different needle sizes. If the stitch pattern is stocking stitch, it is not unusual to find that either the knit or purl row is slightly looser or tighter than it should be. Choose the appropriate needle size, one size up or down, for the stitch problem.

FINAL CHECK

Continue to work tension swatches until a swatch with the correct stitch count has been worked. As a final check, this swatch should be washed, dried and measured again. The fabric's durability and drape can also be assessed at this stage.

ASSESSING THE FABRIC

If the tension is that suggested by a pattern, it should look like the sample in the photograph, but you can still make adjustments if it doesn't meet your expectations. Work another swatch, adjusting the tension as appropriate and treat the new fabric as a yarn substitution (see Substituting Yarns on page 18). If the tension is that of the ball band, then the tension is probably that of a fairly average fabric and may require further adjustment for a lighter, lacy fabric or a firm edging. Continue to work the swatch until the fabric is perfect.

This process should be repeated for each type of yarn used in a project. Luckily, in the case of block blankets, the tension swatch could be a worked block and if only small adjustments are required, these may eventually become part of the blanket.

△ **Checking a square**
Always check that a block is exactly square if you are using it as part of a blanket design. (For this block pattern see page 104.)
1 Knit (or crochet) the suggested number of rows for the block pattern.
2 To check the swatch is square, fold the bottom right corner to the top of the last row worked so the right edge runs along the top of the last row of stitches. If the swatch is square, the bottom right corner will meet the top left corner of the swatch exactly.

A sample being weighed on postage scales.

TIP

For yarns where it is difficult to count the stitches, such as mohair and novelty yarns, loop a short length of thread around the bar between two stitches every two or three stitches along the middle row.

CALCULATING YARN QUANTITY

With a large project that might take several months to complete, it is always a good idea to figure the yarn quantity, as the yarn might not be available later on.

1 Measure the total height and width of the swatch and weigh it. Divide the depth and width of the proposed blanket by the depth and width of the swatch to a couple of decimal places.

2 Multiply these two numbers together to find the total number of similar sized blocks in the blanket, then multiply the weight of the swatch by this number to calculate the total weight of yarn required.

3 Divide this total by the weight of one ball to arrive at the number of balls required to complete the blanket. If more than one colour or yarn is being used, then calculate the percentage of each by looking at the pattern repeats.

• If the swatch is a block sample, weigh the block and multiply the weight by the number of similar blocks. Divide this by the weight of one ball to calculate the number of balls.

• If the swatch has beads, weigh fifty or more, and divide the total weight by the number of beads to find the weight of each bead. Multiply this by the number of beads in the swatch, and subtract this figure from the swatch weight.

STANDARD BED AND BLANKET SIZES

It is now time to find out what is involved in making a blanket. Having the right information makes completing your project more manageable.

BLANKET MEASUREMENTS

Making a blanket will always be a big project, requiring a lot of time and a lot of yarn. However, if you complete only one block each day, then even the largest project will take less than eight months, and if the blocks are interesting and varied, it won't become a chore. It is, after all, potentially an heirloom in the making.

The same long-term reasoning can be applied to the purchase of yarn. Choose the yarn carefully. Remember that although yarn is sold by weight, cotton weighs more than the wool equivalent, and it is the yardage that determines how many stitches a ball of yarn will make. So 50g (1¾oz) of DK-weight cotton may only be 114m (125yd), the same

quantity and weight in wool 119m (130yd), and a cashmere mix 128m (140yd). The lowest yardages are often found in novelty yarns. A little bit of luxury can go a long way, especially if mixed with cheaper yarns, but novelty yarns are not always durable.

There are very few certainties in making a blanket, and the following figures are only a guide. Always double check that the bed is, in fact, a standard size, calculate the yarn quantities carefully (see page 15), and buy slightly more yarn than you think you'll need

to allow for any ideas you may have along the way. A matching cushion or two, for example, will always be useful.

THROW MEASUREMENTS

There are no standard measurements for making a throw. They tend to be a heavier weight than a shawl, and between a blanket and a shawl in size. To calculate the size of a throw, consider the following: the average distance from waist to ground for an adult is about 80cm (32in) – about six blocks; the average distance around the shoulders with a comfortable overlap is about 152cm (60in) – about ten blocks. But there are no hard-and-fast rules. For a chair throw, start by measuring the width and the depth of the chair, the distance from the seat to the top of the back, and then to the ground or from the ground to the arm, from the arm to the seat, across the seat to the other arm, and up and over the arm back to the ground.

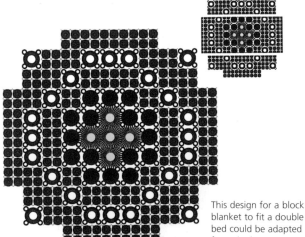

This design for a block blanket to fit a double bed could be adapted for a single.

STANDARD BED AND QUILT SIZES

BED	MATTRESS SIZE	QUILT SIZE*	BLOCKS**	BLOCK TOTAL
Crib	58 x 117cm (23 x 46in)	90 x 135cm (36 x 54in)	6 x 9	54
Buggy blanket (not standardized)		105–150cm (42–60in square)	7–10 square	49–100
Single	99 x 190cm (39 x 75in)	135 x 210cm (54 x 84in)	9 x 14	126
Double	135 x 190cm (54 x 75in)	165 x 210cm (66 x 84in)	11 x 14	154
Queen	150 x 200cm (60 x 80in)	180 x 225cm (72 x 90in)	12 x 15	180
King	193 x 200cm (76 x 80in)	225 x 225cm (90 x 90in)	15 x 15	225

* Mattress size plus a 15-cm (6-in) overhang on three sides. This number has been made to be divisible by whole blocks.
** Based on 15-cm (6-in) square blocks.

AMOUNT OF YARN REQUIRED

There are four main variables: the fibre's relative weight to other fibres, the yarn weight, the density of the fabric and whether a blanket is knitted or crocheted. To eliminate the first variable, the figures are given in yards (not by weight), then to simplify what can only be a rough guide, only three fabric densities are given – lightweight, mediumweight and heavyweight. These will vary depending on the tension and stitch pattern. Remember that a block or a multicoloured blanket will require more yarn than an all-in-one piece.

CROCHETED

Fabric:	Lightweight	Mediumweight	Heavyweight
Crib			
Superfine	2,100–3,100m (2,300–3,300yd)	3,100–3,400m (3,300–3,700yd)	
Fine	1,500–2,200m (1,600–2,400yd)	2,200–3,100m (2,400–3,400yd)	
Light	1,300–1,800m (1,300–2,000yd)	1,800–2,200m (2,000–2,400yd)	2,200–3,900m (2,400–4,300yd)
Medium	900–1,300m (900–1,400yd)	1,300–1,800m (1,400–2,000yd)	1,800–3,200m (2,000–3,500yd)
Bulky	600–900m (600–1,000yd)	900–1,300m (1,000–1,400yd)	1,300–2,400m (1,400–2,500yd)
Super bulky	400–600m (400–600yd)	600–900m (600–1,000yd)	
Single			
Superfine	4,000–7,100m (5,400–7,800yd)	7,100–7,800m (7,800–8,500yd)	
Fine	3,500–5,100m (3,800–5,600yd)	5,100–7,100m (5,600–7,800yd)	
Light	2,800–4,100m (3,100–4,500yd)	4,100–5,100m (4,500–5,600yd)	5,100–10,000m (5,600–10,000yd)
Medium	2,000–2,900m (2,000–3,200yd)	2,900–4,100m (3,200–4,500yd)	4,100–7,400m (4,500–8,000yd)
Bulky	1,400–2,000m (1,500–2,200yd)	2,000–2,900m (2,200–3,200yd)	2,900–5,300m (3,200–5,800yd)
Super bulky	900–1,300m (900–1,400yd)	1,300–2,000m (1,400–2,200yd)	
Double			
Superfine	6,000–8,700m (6,600–9,500yd)	8,700–9,500m (9,500–10,400yd)	
Fine	4,300–6,200m (4,700–6,800yd)	6,200–8,700m (6,800–9,600yd)	
Light	3,400–5,000m (3,800–5,500yd)	5,000–6,200m (5,500–6,800yd)	6,200–11,100m (6,800–13,000yd)
Medium	2,400–3,600m (2,700–3,900yd)	3,600–5,000m (3,900–5,500yd)	5,000–9,000m (5,500–9,900yd)
Bulky	1,600–2,400m (1,800–2,600yd)	2,400–3,600m (2,600–3,900yd)	3,600–6,400m (3,900–7,000yd)
Super bulky	1,000–1,600m (1,100–1,800yd)	1,600–2,400m (1,800–2,600yd)	
Queen			
Superfine	7,000–10,200m (7,700–11,100yd)	10,200–11,100m (11,100–12,200yd)	
Fine	5,100–7,300m (5,500–8,000yd)	7,300–10,200m (1,500–11,100yd)	
Light	4,000–5,900m (4,400–6,500yd)	5,900–7,300m (6,500–8,000yd)	7,300–13,000m (8,000–14,300yd)
Medium	2,800–4,200m (3,100–4,600yd)	4,200–5,900m (4,600–6,500yd)	5,900–10,500m (6,500–11,600yd)
Bulky	1,900–2,800m (2,100–3,000yd)	2,800–4,200m (3,000–4,600yd)	4,200–7,500m (4,600–8,200yd)
Super bulky	1,200–1,900m (1,400–2,000yd)	1,900–2,800m (2,000–3,100yd)	
King			
Superfine	8,800–12,700m (9,700–13,900yd)	12,700–13,800m (13,900–15,200yd)	
Fine	6,300–9,000m (6,900–9,900yd)	9,000–12,700m (9,900–13,900yd)	
Light	5,100–7,300m (5,600–8,000yd)	7,300–9,100m (8,000–9,900yd)	9,100–16,300m (9,900–17,900yd)
Medium	3,700–5,200m (3,900–5,700yd)	5,200–7,300m (5,700–8,000yd)	7,300–13,200m (8,000–14,500yd)
Bulky	2,400–3,500m (2,600–3,800yd)	3,500–5,200m (3,800–5,700yd)	5,200–9,400m (5,700–10,300yd)
Super bulky	1,500–2,300m (1,700–2,500yd)	2,300–3,500m (2,500–3,800yd)	

KNITTED

Fabric:	Lightweight	Mediumweight	Heavyweight
Crib			
Superfine	1,600–2,400m (1,700–2,600yd)	2,400–2,600m (2,600–2,800yd)	
Fine	1,100–1,700m (1,200–1,900yd)	1,700–2,400m (1,900–2,600yd)	
Light	1,000–1,400m (1,000–1,500yd)	1,400–1,700m (1,500–1,900yd)	1,700–3,000m (1,900–3,300yd)
Medium	700–1,000m (700–1,000yd)	1,000–1,400m (1,000–1,500yd)	1,400–2,500m (1,500–2,700yd)
Bulky	500–700m (500–700yd)	700–1,000m (700–1,000yd)	1,000–1,800m (1,000–1,800yd)
Super bulky	300–500m (300–500yd)	500–700m (500–700yd)	
Single			
Superfine	3,900–5,500m (4,100–6,000yd)	5,500–6,000m (6,000–6,600yd)	
Fine	2,800–3,900m (3,000–4,300yd)	3,900–5,500m (4,300–6,000yd)	
Light	2,200–3,200m (2,400–3,500yd)	3,200–3,900m (3,500–4,300yd)	3,900–7,000m (4,300–7,700yd)
Medium	1,600–2,300m (1,700–2,500yd)	2,300–3,200m (2,500–3,500yd)	3,200–5,700m (3,200–5,700yd)
Bulky	1,100–1,500m (1,100–1,700yd)	1,500–2,300m (1,700–2,500yd)	2,300–4,100m (2,500–4,400yd)
Super bulky	700–1,000m (700–1,000yd)	1,000–1,500m (1,000–1,700yd)	
Double			
Superfine	4,700–6,700m (5,100–7,400yd)	6,700–7,300m (7,400–8,000yd)	
Fine	3,400–4800m (3,600–5,200yd)	4,800–6,700m (5,200–7,400yd)	
Light	2,700–3,900m (2,900–4,300yd)	3,900–4,800m (4,300–5,200yd)	4,800–8,600m (5,200–9,400yd)
Medium	2,000–2,800m (2,000–3,000yd)	2,800–3,900m (3,000–4,300yd)	3,900–7,000m (4,300–7,600yd)
Bulky	1,300–1,900m (1,300–2,000yd)	1,900–2,800m (2,000–3,000yd)	5,200–9,400m (3,000–5,400yd)
Super bulky	900–1,200m (900–1,400yd)	1,200–1,900m (1,400–2,000yd)	
Queen			
Superfine	5,500–7,800m (5,900–8,600yd)	7,800–8,500m (8,600–9,400yd)	
Fine	3,900–5,600m (4,200–6,000yd)	5,600–7,800m (6,000–8,600yd)	
Light	3,200–4,500m (3,400–5,000yd)	4,500–5,600m (5,000–6,000yd)	5,600–10,000m (6,000–11,000yd)
Medium	2,300–3,200m (2,400–3,500yd)	3,200–4,500m (3,500–5,000yd)	4,500–8,100m (5,000–8,900yd)
Bulky	1,500–2,200m (1,600–2,400yd)	2,200–3,200m (2,400–3,500yd)	5,200–9,400m (3,500–6,300yd)
Super bulky	1,000–1,500m (1,000–1,500yd)	1,500–2,200m (1,500–2,400yd)	
King			
Superfine	6,900–9,800m (7,400–10,700yd)	9,800–10,700m (10,700–11,700yd)	
Fine	4,900–7,000m (5,300–7,700yd)	7,000–9,800m (7,700–10,700yd)	
Light	4,000–5,700m (4,300–6,200yd)	5,700–7,000m (6,200–7,700yd)	7,000–12,500m (7,700–13,800yd)
Medium	2,800–4,000m (3,000–4,400yd)	4,000–5,700m (4,400–6,200yd)	5,700–10,100m (6,200–11,100yd)
Bulky	1,900–2,700m (2,000–3,000yd)	2,700–4,000m (3,000–4,400yd)	4,000–7,200m (4,400–7,900yd)
Super bulky	1,300–1,800m (1,400–2,000yd)	1,800–2,700m (2,000–3,000yd)	

5 SUBSTITUTING YARNS

If you want to design your own project, or discover that a yarn used for a great project has been discontinued, then knowing how to substitute yarns is a useful technique.

You may have the perfect yarn but no pattern to work with, or the perfect pattern but discover that the yarn is no longer available. The answer is to find the perfect pattern and the perfect yarn, and marry them together.

ALL-IN-ONE PIECE BLANKET

Substituting yarn is simple with an all-in-one piece blanket pattern. Although beds come in standard sizes, a few centimetres difference in size either way won't matter. Start by working a tension swatch in the stitch pattern using the needles suggested on the ball band. Assess the fabric and, if no further tension adjustments are required, count the number of stitches and rows over a distance of 10cm (4in), then divide this figure by ten. This gives an accurate stitch count per centimetre. Multiply the width of the blanket in in by the stitch count per cm and adjust this total to suit the stitch pattern repeat.

BLOCK BLANKET

If the blanket is to be made up of blocks, start by determining the tension of the yarn and

working a block as stated in the pattern, but with the needles suggested on the ball band. If the fabric feels good but the block is the wrong size, then you can either work slightly smaller or larger blocks, and make more or fewer of them. Alternatively, look at the block design and add or remove stitches from the edges, or reduce or increase the number of pattern repeats, or both. Drawing a chart may make this easier (see Charting Ideas, page 32).

DESIGNING YOUR OWN

For both all-in-one and block blankets, make a swatch to calculate the amount of yarn required (see page 15). Start by working a swatch in the chosen yarn in a variety of stitches. Rib, stocking stitch and seed stitch are good stitch patterns to start with. It is also a good idea to see how the yarn will react to yarnovers and multiple decreases. Consider the yarn objectively – do the stitch patterns stand out? Was it easy to work? – then look again for a suitable pattern. Remember that designing a blanket from scratch gets around the yarn "problem" by giving you complete control over the design.

TIP

If the proposed substituted yarn is a lighter weight than that required by the pattern, try using two strands or mixing it with another yarn, such as mohair.

△ **Big and chunky**
Although the tension of this swatch is good because the motif is not too stiff and it holds its shape, you will need to ensure that when it is joined to the other motifs the size of the gap between each motif will not be impractical. If it is a "love the yarn" situation, then one solution would be to find a smaller motif to fit in the spaces between the large motifs.

△ **Fine and fluffy**
The detail of the stitching in the swatch above is lost, and for anything bigger than a crib blanket this would be a labour of love. It would make a lovely motif applied into a larger block.

WRAPS PER INCH (WPI)

This term refers to the number of times a length of yarn can be wrapped around a straight edge, such as a ruler, with each strand sitting comfortably next to the last, not being stretched, within the distance of an inch. It measures the physical width of a strand but says very little about the nature of the yarn. What it does do is give an indication of the number of yards a ball of yarn will contain for a given weight.

Yarn weight	Stitch tension per in	Wraps per in	Metres per 50g
Superfine	6½–8	16–18	146–228
Fine	6–6½	14–15	128–137
Light	5–6	12–13	119–128
Medium	4–5	10–11	82–119
Bulky	3–4½	8–9	46–82
Super bulky	1½–3	up to 7	up to 46

▷ **Bright and beautiful**
Multicoloured yarns are a wonderful way to get a range of colours into a project without all those ends to sew in. However, their unpredictable nature, although exciting, can make the overall design look confusing. If the yarn has a stripe repeat, then starting at the same point or a series of fixed points for each new motif or range of motifs will help.

△ **Winding for wraps per inch (wpi)**
Two yarns – one mohair (above left), one wool (above right) – may have the same wpi count, but the mohair will benefit from a larger needle or hook size because it is difficult to accommodate the hairy nature of the yarn in this kind of measure.

PLY

The lightest yarn is a single length of twisted yarn – one-ply. Two-ply is two twisted lengths twisted together to create a thicker and stronger yarn, and so it continues. However, it is possible to have a chunky yarn with only two or three plies and a finer yarn with four plies. The chunky yarn and the plies within it may be more loosely spun and contain more air. Very loosely spun yarn can break more easily as it is worked and a blanket will rely more on the strength of the fibre or stitch to give it durability. However, yarn with fewer plies will drape better than an equivalent yarn weight with more plies.

DESIGNING BLANKETS
AND
THROWS

●

Following a pattern is a relatively safe route, but for a project as large as a blanket or throw it is still a good idea to have a basic knowledge of the points to consider before embarking on such a big project. And if this knowledge encourages you to experiment along the way, well, who said knitting and crochet isn't exciting?

See page 6 for a key to the symbols used.

6 DESIGNING WITH COLOUR

Colour is an essential element of blanket design, but working out how to use it best can be challenging.

More than one colour can appear together in the form of stripes, in stitch patterns, Fair Isle, or in blocks as intarsia knitting or jacquard crochet. These techniques open up a world of imagery on the right side of the blanket, though the effect on the reverse may not always be desirable.

KNITTING IN COLOUR

Most knitted colour motifs and images are done in stocking stitch, which has a right and a wrong side. A blanket with a stitch pattern with a right and a wrong side will also have a right and a wrong side; unless it is made up of blocks with the right and wrong sides alternated (you will need to have an impeccable knitting technique to make this method look attractive).

The alternative to living with a right and wrong side is to use stitch patterns that incorporate the different coloured strands of yarn into the design and repeat them on both sides of the work (see page 81).

CROCHET IN COLOUR

In crochet, the use of colour and the wrong side is less of a problem than in knitting, as strands of yarn can easily be stitched over. The stitches do differ on the right side and the wrong side, but the difference is subtle. Coloured crochet has the added advantage over knitting in that it is easier to keep both sides neat and unstretched. There is no balancing of two needles while the correct strand of yarn is sought at the back of the work. Again, there are numerous possible stitch patterns that may not be the same on both sides but certainly look very presentable (see pages 36–39).

STRIPES FOR ALL

Stripes are the hero of blanket design. They have all their stranding along the edges which can easily be hidden in a crochet seam, they can use up all those odd balls left from past projects, and they can link the colours of different blanket blocks to unify a blanket design.

RIGHT SIDE OF INTARSIA

It is difficult to keep more complex intarsia designs, such as the one shown below, neat on the wrong side. Even if the knitting is completed successfully the number of ends to be woven in may prove too much. The solution may be to back the finished blanket with fabric or another knitted block.

▽ ▷ **Weaving in ends**
Simple intarsia shapes have a naive charm on the reverse if the ends are woven in carefully and follow the line of the stitching.

BACKWARDS AND FORWARDS OR ROUND AND ROUND

One of the lovely things about crochet blanket blocks is that they can be worked backwards and forwards with no shaping or counting. Working from the centre or corner of a motif will involve increases or decreases, but the motif shape and edgings have a consistent form and in the case of this circle, there are few colour changes.

Use a blunt tapestry needle to weave in ends on the reverse of intarsia knitting.

STRANDED KNITTING OR INTARSIA?

Incorporating colour into knitting requires one of two techniques: stranded knitting or intarsia. The one you choose depends on the size of the motif and the effect you would like to achieve on the reverse of the work. In general, stranded knitting is used for small motifs such as those in Fair Isle designs, while intarsia is suitable for larger areas of colour.

△ **Blocks of colour**
The right side of the knitted motif. The stocking stitch forms neat blocks of colour.

△ **The possibilities of strands**
The strands of yarn on the reverse have a beauty of their own, and huge design possibilities. For a blanket these strands must be kept short as they have a tendency to snag and pull.

KNITTED CIRCLE MOTIF

A circle motif is a very useful addition to a knitted motif library. The shape is simple enough to look good on both sides and it is easy to memorize.

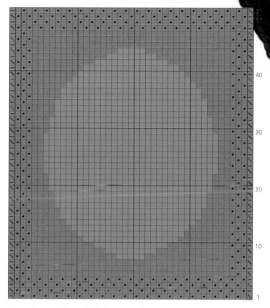

Chart for stocking stitch circle motif

◁ △ **Adding extra colour**
This stocking stitch block was knitted following the chart shown on the left. Variegated yarn adds extra colour without the need for yarn changes, minimizing extra bulk and ends to weave in.

CROCHET CIRCLE MOTIF

There are endless possibilities once the basic outline of a circle is established and, like all motifs, it can be repeated across a blanket using up scraps of yarn. In addition to dividing the circle, try counting stitches in from the outline to create concentric circles.

This double crochet block with a divided circle motif was adapted from the chart shown above.

Chart for double crochet circle motif

CHOOSING COLOURS

Making colour choices is supposedly the decision that knitters and crocheters fear most. There are no hard and fast rules about colour, but a colour wheel will help you in decision making.

Choosing colours for a project can be complicated because so many factors have a bearing on the outcome. Whether or not your blanket is in fashion is unimportant because it will be an heirloom and will endure beyond the limits of fashion. At more than one point in its existence it will be fashionable. In the confines of your room, it will either be an accent and a focal point, or blend seamlessly into the overall scheme of your decor.

▽ Purse-size shopping guides
Colour test strips can act as a guide when you are in a store purchasing the yarn for a project.

COLOUR COMBINATIONS

All around you, colours co-exist with each other, and their peculiarities are used to advantage on everything from wall coverings to food packaging. However, there is a useful trick to be learned here. If a ball of yarn draws your attention more than another but you are not sure if it is suitable for your project, think back to the time you have seen that colour before and what other colours were with it.

While you are out and about, look out for interesting colour combinations and note the proportions of the colours as this will have a bearing on the success of your choice. A sketchbook or scrapbook can be very useful, and you can also study the position of interesting colour combinations on an artist's colour wheel (see below). A pattern or sequence of colours can then be applied to another palette with equal success, so don't just look for inspiration in the palette of colours you have planned for your next project.

△ Explore colour
It is always useful to experiment with colours that wouldn't be your first choice with other colours you have chosen – if only to eliminate them once and for all – but it is surprising how often they become part of the final scheme.

TEST STRIPS

Winding yarn around a strip of cardboard can be a useful tool. Take a piece of cardboard about 2.5cm (1in) wide. Hold a crochet hook with a slip knot on it against one edge. Wrap the yarn around the cardboard and back to the edge, yarn over hook, and slip stitch the wrap in place. Repeat along the edge of the cardboard, joining in new yarn as required. Yarn can then be placed over the wrapped yarn or, using a tapestry needle, woven through it. Raid your yarn stash or buy small quantities of tapestry wool and experiment not only with the colours but also the colour proportions until you are happy.

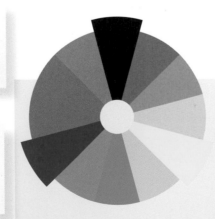

ARTIST'S COLOUR WHEEL

The basic colour wheel is made up of three primary colours – red, blue and yellow. Adjoining colours are mixed to create the secondary colours and these are mixed with their neighbours to create tertiary colours. Adjacent colours are harmonious. Colours opposite each other are called complementary colours – they have no tones in common. Complementaries together create clashing, vibrant combinations.

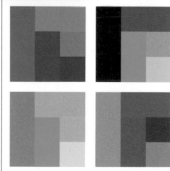

△ ▷ Using the colour wheel

Colours are selected around the colour wheel, at the same intervals as the colours of the original palette. Reversing the proportions of the colours creates a different visual impression. For the pattern see page 72.

△ Transposing colours

In image **a**, neither the colour of the bird nor the background shapes dominate. Either can be made more dominant by using a warmer or darker coloured yarn (as seen in **b**). Choosing a yarn with more of a third primary colour or black, will help to make the areas of colour more distinct. In **c**, a yarn with more yellow has been substituted for one of the yarns in each scheme, making the blue slightly more green and the pink more orange. For the pattern, see page 103.

△ Complementary and harmonious colours

A small amount of a complementary colour can be a useful focal point. The brown and purple in this swatch are tonally the same, but their visual impact is different. For pattern, see first stage of adapted rib, page 34.

△ Sari inspiration

A sari fabric inspired the colours and the proportions in this block. The stripes are worked in treble crochet, double crochet, and half-treble crochet worked into the back loop only. Although it is a block, the top third could be the start of a new repeat as the sequence is the same as that of the bottom third but with two colours changed.

8 READING CHARTS

Reading a chart or diagram is easy when you know how, and is a useful skill when you are choosing and designing patterns.

There are several different kinds of charts – check the instructions on how to read each new pattern chart, as they do vary, but basically the following rules apply.

SQUARED CHARTS

For knit or crochet, start by casting on or working a foundation chain as instructed, then work the pattern as directed by the key and accompanying notes, starting at the bottom right of the chart. One square usually represents one stitch, but in some cases, such as increases, the symbols represent an action and more than one stitch loop or, in the case of filet charts, a solid mesh square represents two stitches. Work from right to left on odd-numbered rows, joining in new colours as required, or carrying out the instructions as described. Even-numbered rows are worked from left to right, and the work progresses from the bottom of the chart to the top.

COLOUR PATTERNS

Each square represents a stitch and a colour. Take care to note any additional instructions in the key. Use new lengths of yarn for each new large area of colour. To avoid holes between two blocks of colour, the yarn just worked should be placed over new yarn to be used at each colour block change. If the distance between stitches of the same colour is short, then the same length of yarn can be used for both areas, but this will leave a strand of yarn on the back of the block. To hide this strand, on the next row, place the strand along the top of the stitches and encase the strand in the new stitches. This method of hiding strands can also be used to avoid weaving in the ends.

In crochet, new colours are added at the last stage of the stitch before the square of the new colour. The last stage of a stitch forms the top of the next stitch.

If the distance between stitches of the same colour is short, then use a single length of yarn and strand across the back of the stitches in between. This will leave a strand of yarn on the back of the block. To hide this strand, place it across the top of the stitches to be worked and encase the strand in the new stitches. This method can also be used to avoid weaving in the ends.

TEXTURED STITCH PATTERNS

Each square represents a stitch and an action, but the principles are the same. Read logically backwards and forwards across the rows, following each action in sequence. Note not only the action, but also the stitch below as this will help you to recognize an error when the pattern is repeated.

CROCHET MOTIF CHARTS

Start by working a foundation chain as instructed and joining with a slip stitch, then work the motif as directed, starting from the centre of the chart and working outwards in an anticlockwise direction. Each symbol represents a stitch or a series of stitches – they are not just confined by the grid.

READING A KNIT COLOUR CHART

This stocking stitch chart requires at least six lengths of yarn. Wind one yellow, two red and two green lengths onto shuttles, and one green straight from the ball.

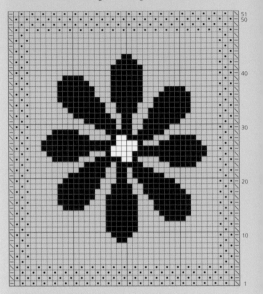

⊠	ktbl in green
☐	p on the RS, k on the WS, in green
⊡	k on the RS, p on the WS, in green
⊟	Yarn to the front, st purlwise
■	p on the RS, k on the WS, in red
☐	k on the RS, p on the WS, in yellow

Cast on 43 sts, in this case using the thumb method, and work row 1, reading from the right, as follows: k1tbl, *k1, p1, rep from * to the end the last 2sts, k1, slip the last st purlwise with the yarn in front.
Row 2: reading from the left, as follows: k1tbl, *k1, p1, rep from * to the end the last 2sts, k1, slip the last st purlwise with the yarn in front. The dot now represents a knit stitch because it is a wrong side row.
Rows 3–4: repeat rows 1–2.
Rows 5: k1tbl, k1, p1, knit to the last 3sts, p1, k1, slip the last st purlwise with the yarn in front.
Rows 6: k1tbl, k1, p1, k1, purl to the last 4sts, k1, p1, k1, slip the last st purlwise with the yarn in front.
Rows 7–8: repeat rows 5–6.
Row 9: k1tbl, k1, p1, k18 in green, join in a length of red yarn and k2sts, join in a second length of green and k16sts, p1, k1, slip the last st purlwise with the yarn in front. Continue in this manner until the chart image has been completed.

This selvedge stitch produces a chain edge, which makes seaming, and particularly crochet seaming, easier.

Row 23 is worked with seven lengths of yarn hanging off the back of the work. This means there are numerous ends to weave in, which will add bulk to the fabric, and the back of the work is less likely to be attractive.

This selvedge stitch works best when the stitch after and before the end stitches are knit stitches.

Clothes pegs make useful bobbins for longer lengths of yarn. Plastic clothes pegs are lighter.

READING A CROCHET MOTIF CHART

These often look more daunting than a knitting pattern. However, once crochet charts have been mastered, they are quicker and easier to follow. This medallion uses three colours, one in each of three rounds.

Rnd 1

Rnd 2

Rnd 3

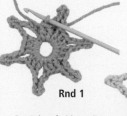

Don't be afraid to adjust the number of chains between stitches. The tension of a chain can vary more than other stitches.

Using yarn A make a slip knot.
Foundation chain: ch 9 and join with a sl st to form a ring. Reading from the centre out and counterclockwise:
Rnd 1 (RS): ch 10 (counts as 1 tr and half a picot) *sl st into the ch 5 chs from the hook (this completes a picot), ch 2, 3 tr into the centre of the ring, ch 7 rep from * five more times, sl st into the ch 5 chs from the hook, ch 2, 2 tr into the centre of the ring, join with a sl st into the 3rd ch of beg ch. Fasten off yarn.

Rnd 2: join in yarn B to a picot sp, ch 10 (1 tr and half a picot) *sl st into the ch 5 chs from the hook, ch 2, 3 tr into the picot, *ch 1, 3 tr into the appointed sp, ch 7, sl st into the ch 5 chs from the hook, ch 2, 3 tr in next picot (this is a star point), rep from * five more times, 2 tr into the next picot, join with a sl st into the 3rd ch of beg ch. Fasten off yarn.
Rep rnd 2 but ch 3, 1 ttr into the next ch, ch 3, between each star point. Fasten off yarn.
Blocks can be joined in rnd 3 by joining picots on adjacent squares with sl sts.

For a pieced sample see page 47.

KEY

◯ foundation chain	⊤ tr in yellow
⬭ ch in yellow	⊤ tr in pale blue
⬭ ch in pale blue	⊤ tr in blue
⬭ ch in blue	⊤ tr in blue
• ss in yellow	
• ss in pale blue	≁ ttr in blue
• ss in blue	

▲ starting point   ▲ fasten off yarn

△ join in new yarn

STRIPES OF COLOUR

Thick, thin, textured, flat, radiating or backwards and forwards – stripes are perfect for blankets.

In the best tradition of the scrap quilt or blanket, stripes are the perfect way to use up odds and ends of yarns from completed projects and for linking colours from one block to another. If you mix in enough colours, stripes will always look good, whatever the reason behind them.

HORIZONTAL STRIPES

The simplest form of stripe is made up of an equal number of rows of two or more colours. If the number of rows in each stripe is an even number and only a few colours are being used, the yarn not in use can be twisted around the working yarn at the end of every second row and stranded up the edge in preparation for its next stripe. The deeper the stripes, the more distinct they will appear; the narrower the stripes, the more they will appear to blend together.

VERTICAL STRIPES

Vertical stripes are also very effective, although the yarn either has to be stranded from one colour group to the next or an intarsia technique must be used. In the case of knitting, working a rib-stitch pattern more than two stitches wide will create a vertical line. The same effect can be achieved in crochet by working longer stitches or stitching around the post.

△ **Striping by numbers**
There are various formulas for finding the ideal depth of a stripe. For example, the Fibonacci sequence, in which the last two numbers in the sequence are added together to make a third: 1, 2, 3, 5, 8 and so on.
    The row count in the swatch shown above follows the Fibonacci number sequence. Deep seed stitch side borders were added to make the centre blocks appear more square.

SINGLE ROW STRIPES

Working a two-colour sequence of single-row stripes can be awkward (especially in knitting, right) because the next stripe colour is always at the "wrong" end. In crochet, simply leave the loop of the last stitch of each row hanging. Then work each colour as required: insert the hook through the loop of the next colour, then work a chain to the height of the top edge of the piece, and a slip stitch into the top of the edge stitch. Finally, work a turning chain and stitches as the pattern states.

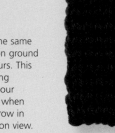

▷ **Colour merging**
Every second stripe is the same colour, giving a common ground to the three other colours. This is a good way of unifying potentially unhappy colour choices but only works when the stripes are very narrow in proportion to the area on view.

▽ **Stripes on a circular needle**
For each colour change, pick up the next colour yarn from whichever end the last stitch was worked, move the stitches along the needle to work from that end and work the row, keeping the pattern correct.

TIP

Ideas for striping sequences include:
• Barcodes on packaging – a mixture of four widths and two colours
• Throws of the dice
• Prime numbers: 1, 3, 5, 7, 11, 13, 17, 19, 23, 31…

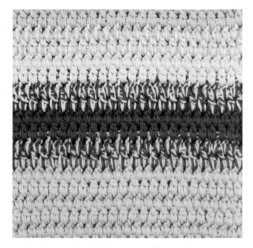

△ Vertical stripes

The variegated yarn was stranded across the back of these vertical stripes. The fabric is not reversible but is attractive on both sides. Experimenting with frequent colour changes within the vertical stripe is well worth the effort.

△ DK and bulky weight stripes

Stripes of different yarn weights are easy to achieve. Work out the tension and the number of stitches for the width for each weight of yarn. On the first row of a new yarn weight stripe, increase or decrease evenly across the row as appropriate.

△ Graduated striping

Two strands of yarn have been used for each stripe to mix the solid colours. This is particularly effective when the colours are very similar but, as you can see, when one colour dominates the transition is less smooth.

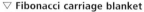

▽ Fibonacci carriage blanket

Fibonacci stripes (see opposite) supposedly make it possible for any colour mix to work beautifully. This blanket has some challenging colour combinations. The original concept was for the striped panels to be pieced together, but the horizontal proportions did not follow the Fibonacci sequence. Plain panels were added for a more harmonious effect.

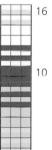

The first stripe has two strands of the first colour, the following stripe has one strand of the first colour and one of the second and the third stripe has two strands of the second colour. The sequence continues with the stripe between each solid block having a strand of each adjacent solid block colour, so creating a mid-colour stripe.

Each square represents one stitch and the colours used. Where two colours are shown within a square, both are used to make one stitch.

16

10

1

TIP

To strand yarn up the side of a work with an odd number of stripe rows, choose an odd number of colours. The stitch pattern can then be worked in the correct row sequence without cutting and joining in yarn for each new stripe or using double-pointed needles.

NOTES

The wrong side of garter stitch has a merging of stripe colours.

In seed stitch, alternate knit and purl stitches are worked across the row and then on subsequent rows the knit stitches of the previous row are purled and the purl stitches of the previous row are knitted. This causes the stitch loop of the row below to appear above that of the colour above on alternate stitches across the row.

TIP

To reduce the appearance of the new colour within the previous stripe in knit and purl stitch patterns, work the first row of a new stripe colour with a smaller needle.

GARTER STITCH

All the rows are knitted but the right and wrong sides look different when stripes are introduced. As you knit, the side facing away from you displays the top of the stitch loop of the previous row above that of the colour you are working with. In the case of a two-row repeat, the second row of the repeat draws up the colour of the row below which is the same colour. So the right side has clearly defined stripes.

For a 15-cm (6-in) block using a DK-weight yarn:
Using yarn A, cast on 36 sts using the thumb method.
Cont to work from the chart.
Rep chart rows until the block measures 15cm (6in) from the cast-on edge.
Cast off.

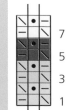

Colours: blue, green, red and yellow
Repeat: 1 st plus selvedge sts

STOCKING STITCH

This block is worked in alternate rows of knit and purl. On the purl side the appearance of the fabric is similar to that of the reverse side of the garter stitch stripe, but on the knit side the stripes are crisper with a smoother texture. The fabric has a slightly better drape than garter stitch, and fewer repeats with less yarn required than that of garter or seed stitch over a similar depth.

For a 15-cm (6-in) block using a DK-weight yarn:
Using yarn A, cast on 36 sts using the thumb method.
Cont to work from the chart.
Rep chart rows until the block measures 15cm (6in) from the cast-on edge.
Cast off.

Colours: blue, green, red and yellow
Repeat: 1 st plus selvedge sts

THREE KNIT, THREE PURL RIB

Groups of knit and purl stitches are worked across the row, but on subsequent rows the knit stitches of the previous row are knitted and the purl stitches of the previous row are purled. This creates vertical bands that appear as stocking stitch and reverse stocking stitch across the row. The drape is better in the direction of the vertical bands than across the vertical bands.

For a 15-cm (6-in) block using a DK-weight yarn:
Using yarn A, cast on 36 sts using the thumb method.
Cont to work from the chart.
Rep chart rows until the block measures 15cm (6in) from the cast-on edge.
Cast off.

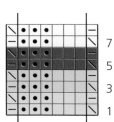

Colours: blue, green, red and yellow
Repeat: 6 sts plus selvedge sts

DOUBLE CROCHET

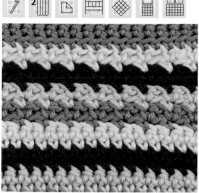

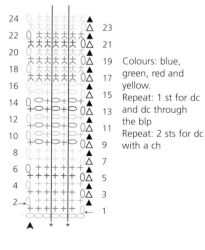

The drape can be improved by chaining a stitch and missing a stitch between each double crochet stitch, or by working into the front or back loops only.

For a 15-cm (6-in) block using a DK-weight yarn:
Foundation chain: using yarn A, ch 29.
Row 1: insert the hook into the 3rd ch from the hook, work 1 dc; this completes the first 2 sts. 1 dc into each ch to the end of the row (28 sts).
Ch 2 (counts as 1 dc) at the beginning of each row, and work the last dc into the bottom of the beg ch before turning.
Cont to work from the chart.
Rep chart rows until the block measures 15cm (6in) from the foundation chain. Fasten off.

Colours: blue, green, red and yellow.
Repeat: 1 st for dc and dc through the blp
Repeat: 2 sts for dc with a ch

TR INTO A STITCH

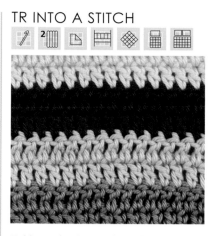

Treble crochet into each stitch works well as a stripe; the drape is good and progress is fast. A slight ridge is formed on the side facing you as you work, which then appears on alternate rows.

For a 15-cm (6-in) block using a DK-weight yarn:
Foundation chain: using yarn A, ch 30.
Row 1: insert the hook into the 4th ch from the hook, work 1 tr; this completes the first 2 sts. 1 tr into each ch to the end of the row (28 sts). Turn.
Ch 2 (counts as 1 tr) at the beginning of each row, and work the last tr into the 2nd ch of the beg ch before turning.
Cont to work from the chart.
Rep chart rows until the block measures 15cm (6in) from the foundation chain. Fasten off.

Colours: blue, green, red and yellow
Repeat: 1 st

TR INTO A SPACE

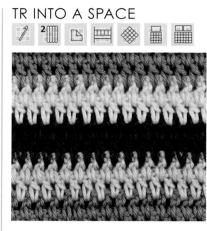

Treble crochet into spaces produces a slightly denser fabric than treble crochet into stitches. The overlapping stitches interrupt the straight stripe edge.

For a 15-cm (6-in) block using a DK-weight yarn:
Foundation chain: using yarn A, ch 30.
Row 1: insert the hook into the 4th ch from the hook, work 1 tr; this completes the first 2 sts. 1 tr into each ch to the end of the row (28 sts). Turn.
Ch 2 (counts as 1 tr) at the beginning of each row, and work the last tr into the last sp before beg ch. Fasten off.
Cont to work from the chart.
Rep chart rows until the block measures 15cm (6in) from the foundation chain. Fasten off.

Colours: blue, green, red and yellow
Repeat: 1 st

VARIATIONS

Treble crochet with front post stitches around a stitch in a row below works well as a stripe. The odd number of colours worked over an even number of stripes within a repeat means that the front post stitches alternate their position each time the colour is used.

In this pattern, treble crochet is worked into each space in the row below it, but in one direction only. In other words, at the end of each row the yarn is fastened off and a new length fastened at the right-hand edge. This is only practical if working on an all-in-one piece blanket, and it does create a slight bias, but it is economical with yarn and has good drape.

CHARTING IDEAS

Having a chart to follow rather than a pattern makes the spacing between stitches easier to see and, for some people, easier to memorize.

Crafters who knit or crochet often say that after a while they can read complex written patterns and visualize accurately how they will look – but when it comes to adapting designs there is nothing quite like having something visual that can be pondered. Even if you design on the needles, creating a chart is a useful way of keeping a record of what has been done and, sometimes more interestingly, what has been discarded. This can often be a source of new ideas.

It can also be fascinating to draw a chart to decipher an unusual stitch pattern. The variations on old ideas that designers use can often be applied to other stitch patterns.

FINDING INSPIRATION

A good place to start is to keep a scrapbook of images, techniques and patterns. Choose images because of their colours, shapes or context of objects. If you chart out the ideas, a stream of inspiration will follow. The elements from several images and ideas often combine for the best ideas.

Look at the work of other artists and crafters. Designs can be copied and translated directly, but also the way ideas are developed can often be adapted to suit knitting and crochet projects.

△ **Printouts from a computer**
There are pros and cons to designing on a computer. It is quick and easy to change and experiment with ideas, but unless new files are constantly saved, good ideas can easily be lost. Print out your ideas; even if they are not what you want to do now, they may be in the future.

◁ **Shade cards**
All spinners produce shade cards for their yarns each season. To keep up to date with an entire collection can be expensive, but they can be purchased and do make designing easier. The colours are often grouped together on the shade card in families of colours that work well together. Cutting up a shade card can seem very drastic but it allows the colours to be mixed and matched more easily.

▷ **Colours**
Shells, flowers, textiles, giftwrap, photographs and packaging can all be a source of colour inspiration. The list is endless. Don't just look at the general overall colour impression, but look closely at objects and at the shades that make up their colour. The popular art school project of examining and painting a 2.5-cm (1-in) square section of an object twelve or fifty times larger is a useful exercise to remember.

DESIGNING COLOUR CHARTS

The simplest form of design is the translation of the colours from one pattern into another palette. Ideally, seek out the yarns and the new colours for a project, even if it is in the form of a series of shade cards. Find suitable colour pencils or colours in a computer palette and redraw the design with the new colours. Continue until the new design is complete, then work a test swatch in the new yarn.

For designing complex colour motifs from scratch, draw a grid of squares, with one square representing one stitch, to the size of the project or block, and sketch in pencil the rough size and placement of the shapes. Remember to allow for seaming. If there is something in the centre squares, the eye will be drawn to this first. From this master it is easy to see how many squares each part of the design will take. Work out the separate areas on separate grids and then transfer them to the master design grid. Adjust the elements so they work well together. If a motif such as a flower is to be repeated several times, it is interesting to alter the image slightly from one repeat to the other.

DESIGNING TEXTURE CHARTS

For designing textured patterns the method of working is similar to that of colour motifs, but when calculating the area and number of stitches, extra care must be taken to compensate for the way that cables and lace affect the width of an area. Plan any repeats carefully. An odd number of repeats will draw the eye to the centre complete repeat in the block. If there is an even number of repeats, the eye will be drawn to the area between two repeats.

REPEATING BLOCKS

If a block is to appear on top of the same block design, start the block halfway through a repeat, plus one row for the seam, and end the block halfway through a repeat, plus one row. The blocks will then appear to run smoothly together. The design will also appear centred vertically within the block. Apply the same rule to blocks placed side by side.

For the more difficult areas, experiment with small swatches and alter the chart if necessary, then work a tension swatch.

CROCHET MEDALLIONS

It can be difficult to chart crochet medallions accurately without good drawing skills or the aid of a graphics program on a computer. One solution is to work or design the pattern in a pale-coloured yarn, photocopy or take a photograph of it against a white background and write a note of the stitches on the paper copy. Do not use white yarn, as too much of the detail will be lost in the reproduction.

CROPPING

Abstract shapes and colours can be isolated by cropping an image using two "L" shapes cut from cardboard. Don't always make the focal point the centre; sometimes a focal point a third in from an edge looks better.

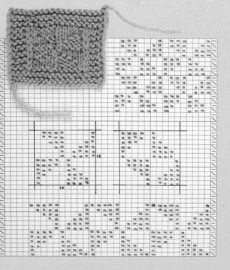

ADAPTING A PATTERN

Drawing a chart is particularly useful if a stitch pattern or block has to be adapted to suit a different yarn, or if a pattern's appearance can be improved or needs to be changed once you have worked a swatch.

Chart out the block or stitch pattern with one square representing one stitch or action, row by row, until the pattern repeat or block has been completed. Any selvedge stitches or spacer stitches that divided columns of a more complex stitch pattern should become clear. Make any adjustments to the chart in a contrasting colour. It is useful to see the original pattern too, but if this is too confusing, redraw the chart. And, of course, work a tension swatch.

11
CROSS-STITCH CHARTS

Cross-stitch charts can be adapted and are a huge
potential resource for knitting and crochet.

Cross-stitch charts are a good design starting
point, but unfortunately knit and crochet
stitches are not square (as cross stitch is).
Cross-stitch designs also usually use more
changes of colours than a knit or crochet
design. However, they are still a good reference
as are bead, tapestry and any other grid images.

ADAPTING FOR KNIT

The most popular stitch pattern to use
for knitted colour work is stocking stitch.
If a complex Fair Isle pattern is worked, its
proportions can approach that of a square,
but the fabric would not have the drape often
desired in a blanket. In the case of stocking
stitch, the height of the stitch is approximately
70 per cent of its width. This means that if a
cross-stitch chart is knitted without any
amendments, the image will be slightly
squashed from top to bottom.

ADAPTING FOR CROCHET

The only crochet stitch that is nearly square
is double crochet, but even that over the depth
of a 15-cm (6-in) square block will squash an
image slightly. However, the distortion will only
be approximately 82 per cent; smaller images
under 20 rows deep can probably be used
without adaptation.
    Two to three consecutive treble crochet
stitches approximately make a square over the
height of one stitch and simple cross-stitch
images can be translated directly into filet
crochet designs (see Filet Lace, page 54).

The cross-stitch chart
Several options are available to an embroiderer that are
not available in knit or crochet. This will impact on design
decisions you must make when adapting a cross-stitch chart.

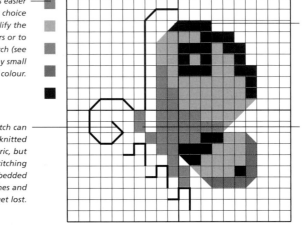

*Changing colours is easier
in embroidery. The choice
is either to simplify the
number of colours or to
use a duplicate stitch (see
page 58) to add any small
or complex areas of colour.*

*Outlines in back stitch can
be reproduced on a knitted
or crocheted fabric, but
vertical lines of stitching
can become embedded
between the stitches and
get lost.*

*Half squares in a cross-
stitch design have to
convert into stitches of
one colour or another.*

*The shape of a knit or
crochet stitch means they
are narrower at the
bottom than the top, so
a stitch placed diagonally
can appear isolated from
the rest of the design.*

TIPS

In order to adapt a cross-stitch chart for knitting or crochet, more
rows have to be added to the design. This is worth calculating
to the exact tension of the proposed fabric.

You can buy plastic grids from hobby stores that can be placed
over an image and used to convert it to squares or stitches of colour.
They are usually intended for cross-stitch design, so the image may
have to be adapted further for knitting or crochet.

Creating a customized grid for the tension of a project is well worth
the effort if there is a lot of colour work to be designed. These can be
hand drawn and then photocopied, or there are sites on the Internet
that will create grids electronically to download. These will give a
truer picture of how a design will look once worked.

Adapting for stocking stitch

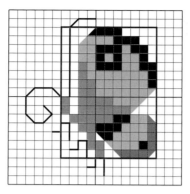

1 Work a tension swatch and count the number of stitches and rows within a 10-cm (4-in) square. If the proposed design will be worked in Fair Isle, add between 10 and 20 per cent to the stitch count, depending on how frequently the colours will change along a row; the more colour changes, the more stitches required. Stranding and weaving yarns creates squarer stitches.

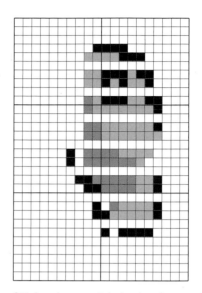

2 To calculate the frequency at which rows must be added to the cross-stitch design to maintain the correct proportions, subtract the number of stitches from the number of rows, then divide this number by the number of stitches. Round to the nearest whole number. For example, if the number is three, you will need to add an extra row every third row.

3 Redraw the cross-stitch chart but after every third row, leave one row empty before continuing to redraw the design. To discover the total number of extra rows over the design, divide the number of rows in the cross-stitch chart by three.

▽ **Working a swatch**
The final stage of a design is to work it. In this swatch, the purple stitches around the wing edges have been worked in duplicate stitch (see page 58) to give a neater and more durable finish.

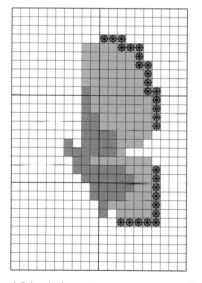

4 Colour in the empty rows as seems appropriate and work a swatch of the image. The position of the extra rows can be adjusted, but the total number of empty rows should remain the same. Check the tension of the new swatch before proceeding with the design.

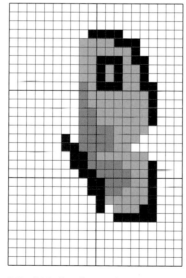

5 The finished stocking stitch chart.

BLOCK DESIGN

When planning block or stitch pattern design, consider the following: the level of skill involved; whether the design will prove either uninteresting or too challenging for the time you have to work on it; whether the drape will be appropriate; the appearance of the design on the reverse; and how the finished piece will endure wear and tear.

Working a tension swatch is always a good idea when selecting a pattern, but it takes time and working through a selection of patterns is not economical. So read through the pattern, check for unfamiliar techniques and try them out on a length of waste yarn; look for clues about the drape and stitch pattern, and then work a select few swatches and wash them several times.

DRAPE

Look at the recommended yarn weight and needle or hook size to see if they match those on page 12. If the needle or hook size is slightly larger, then the drape is likely to be slightly lighter than a fabric you would work for a sweater. Of course, if the pattern is heavily textured, two or more needle or hook sizes bigger may be required to lighten the drape.

REVERSIBILITY

It is difficult to imagine how a stitch pattern will look on the reverse. Often, the right side is shown, but not the reverse. A throw with an unsightly reverse side on display is unattractive. One solution is to look for stitch patterns that have an odd number of row repeats. This means that the first row of a repeat will appear on alternate sides of the work.

DESIGNING REVERSIBLE STITCH PATTERNS

One of the easiest ways of designing a new stitch pattern is to adapt a pattern that already has the characteristics you are looking for.

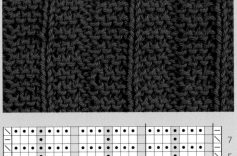

1 This simple rib is reversible and because it ends with a purl stitch will appear as a knit stitch on the other side, identical on both sides. However, because of the way it contracts across its width, it is yarn hungry and time consuming to knit.

2 The rib repeat has been split and moved apart. The area between has been filled with garter stitch, which is identical on both sides and adds width to the stitch pattern. The fabric is still rather dense and uninteresting to work, but an attractive concertina effect has been created.

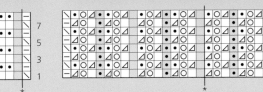

3 A basic lace stitch has been added. The fabric still has the pleated feel, but it is now much lighter. To continue to create a pattern which is identical on both sides, the stitch repeat on the right of a row must be repeated on the left of the row, mirrored from the centre, and as the right-hand side appears, on its reverse side.

FAGGOT STITCH

This simple lace fabric has some stretch and a bias to the right because of the repeated use of the knit-two-together decrease, but this can be eliminated by combining the two-stage action with other stitches – see Step 3 opposite. Working lace stitch patterns with slightly larger needles produces a more pronounced lace effect.

For a 15-cm (6-in) block using a DK-weight yarn:
Using yarn A, cast on 32 sts using the thumb method.
Cont to work from the chart.
Rep chart rows until the block measures 15cm (6in) from the cast-on edge.
Cast off.

Repeat: 2 sts

BRIOCHE STITCH

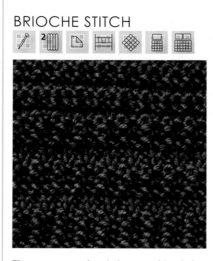

There are several variations on this stitch and it is a popular choice for throws and shawls because its fabric has a depth that traps air. This gives it a lighter drape than its appearance would suggest and also makes it very warm.

For a 15-cm (6-in) block using a DK-weight yarn:
Using yarn A, cast on 36 sts using the thumb method.
Foundation row: *Yo, sl 1 st purlwise, k1* rep from * to * to the end of the row.
Cont to work from the chart.
Rep charts rows until the block measures 15cm (6in) from the cast-on edge.
Cast off.

Repeat: 2 sts

SLIP-STITCH STITCH

Slip-stitch stitch patterns are an excellent way of introducing colour changes to a row without using more than one yarn in any one row. This pattern is an example of how an odd number of rows can produce a reversible fabric. Slip-stitch stitch patterns produce a dense fabric unless they are worked on larger needles than the yarn would normally warrant.

For a 15-cm (6-in) block using a DK-weight yarn:
Using yarn A, cast on 36 sts using the thumb method.
Cont to work from the chart.
Rep charts rows until the block measures 15cm (6in) from the cast-on edge.
Cast off.

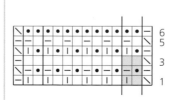

Repeat: 2 sts plus selvedge sts

GARTER STITCH

This is the ultimate one-row repeat. It can be created by either knitting all the rows or purling all the rows. It is reversible and one stitch over two rows forms a square area, which makes it very useful for creating block shapes other than squares. The drape can be heavy if worked on the recommended needles, but it looks good when worked on larger needles. For a neat edge, knit into the back of the first stitch of every row and slip the last stitch of every row purlwise with the yarn in front. This creates a chain edge, which is very useful for working the seams.

KEY

Ⓘ yo, sl 1 st purlwise.

13

STITCH PATTERN BLOCK REPEATS

A stitch pattern can be made reversible by working an odd-row repeat, or by working blocks of stitches on alternate sides of the fabric.

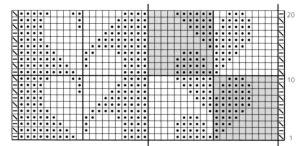

Simple reversible block patterns
The stitch pattern in this block has been mirrored over the centre, both vertically and horizontally. This block is a good standard grid on which to impose stitch patterns and designs. The border is garter stitch.

A blanket block can be further divided into smaller blocks or groups of stitches to create a reversible 15cm (6in) blanket block design. Designing row repeats to create reversible stitch patterns can be developed further by dividing a block into units, which can then be repeated,

rotated and mirrored across a blanket block or a larger area of an all-in-one piece blanket.

This process of manipulating stitch repeats can then be used in a block blanket with the individual blocks, which are in a sense even larger stitch repeats, to create reversible blankets.

MANIPULATING A BLOCK

Each of these designs is drawn on a chart grid. Each square of the grid represents the true proportions of the knit stitch.

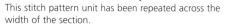

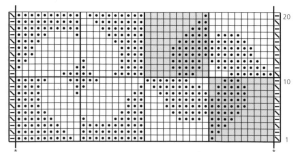

This stitch pattern unit has been repeated across the width of the section.

In this case, the stitch pattern unit has been reversed from front to back facing in every alternate repeat.

The stitch pattern unit has been redrawn to allow for the differing stitch height and width, and rotated.

Different ideas are explored further.

Converting images into texture
The flower image on page 26 has been converted into blocks of knit and purl. The block is not identical on both sides, but is attractive on both sides with one side mirroring the other.

SEED STITCH

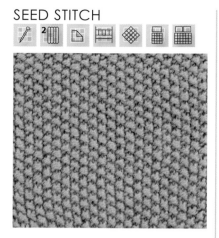

There are two ways of looking at this repeat: first, as a group of four stitches repeated; second, as a knit one, purl one rib with every alternate row moved one repeat stitch to the left. Continuing the repeat for one more stitch would edge the fabric with knit stitches on the right side and purl stitches on the wrong side.

For a 15-cm (6-in) block using a DK-weight yarn:
Cast on 36 sts using the thumb method.
Cont to work from the chart.
Rep chart rows until the block measures 15cm (6in) from the cast-on edge.
Cast off.

Repeat: 2 sts plus selvedge sts

DIAGONAL RIB

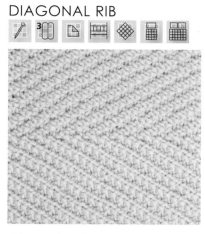

This pattern could be described as an offset rib pattern. It has a four-row repeat that is worked until half the required depth is reached. Then a turning row is worked, shown on the chart as row 5, and a new repeat mirroring that of the repeat before the turning row is worked.

For a 15-cm (6-in) block using a DK-weight yarn:
Cast on 36 sts using the thumb method.
Cont to work from the chart.
Rep chart rows until the block measures 15cm (6in) from the cast-on edge.
Cast off.

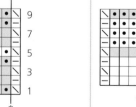

Repeat: 4 sts plus selvedge sts

BASKETWEAVE

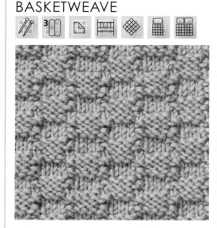

This is a version of basketweave stitch that is reversible. It does not have such a pronounced curve to the blocks of stitches as the traditional basketweave stitch patterns and it takes a little more concentration to knit, but it isn't difficult.

For a 15-cm (6-in) block using a DK-weight yarn:
Cast on 35 sts using the thumb method.
Cont to work from the chart.
Rep chart rows until the block measures 15cm (6in) from the cast-on edge.
Cast off.

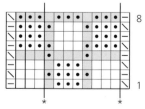

Repeat: 8 sts plus 3 plus selvedge sts

REVERSIBLE BASKETWEAVE

The true basketweave stitch pattern is not reversible.

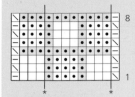

The highlighted stitches appear as purl on the right side of the fabric and knit on the wrong side. They produce the distinctive three-dimensional curved fabric that mimics basketweave.

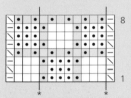

Making the stitches reversible by converting the highlighted areas to seed stitch flattens the fabric and creates a chequerboard pattern with soft edges to the blocks of knit and purl stitches.

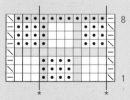

Here, lines of knit stitches are kept in the highlighted areas but half of the stitches are mirrored with purl stitches.

ALTERNATE STITCH HEIGHT MESH

Like most crochet patterns, the alternate double crochet and treble crochet stitch pattern can be adapted and have a lighter drape by skipping a stitch or chain, and adding a chain stitch between each double crochet and treble crochet stitch. Repeat: 4 sts.

TREBLE CROCHET V-SHAPE PATTERN

The beauty of this pattern is that after the first row the hook is inserted into a space to make a stitch. This makes it quicker to work and is a useful consideration when selecting stitch patterns.

For a 15-cm (6-in) square block using a DK-weight yarn:
Foundation chain: ch 31.
Row 1: yo, insert the hook into the 5th ch from the hook, work 1 tr, 1 ch, 1 tr into this ch; this completes the first 3 sts. Cont to work from the chart to the end of the row (29 sts). Turn.
Ch 3 (counts as 1 tr) at the beginning of each row, and work the last tr into the 2nd ch of the beg-ch before turning. Cont to work from the chart.
Rep chart rows until the block measures 15cm (6in) from the foundation chain. Fasten off yarn.

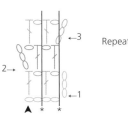

Repeat: 2 sts plus 1 st

TREBLE CROCHET MESH

This stitch pattern is quick and easy to work, with a light drape that can relieve the weight and improve the drape of heavier blocks. It looks good in variegated or space-dyed yarns, but yarns that rely on their texture for interest may not look as attractive.

For a 15-cm (6-in) square block using a DK-weight yarn:
Foundation chain: ch 30.
Row 1: insert the hook into the 6th ch from the hook, work 1 tr; this completes the first st, ch, tr st. Cont to work from the chart to the end of the row (14 tr sts). Turn.
Ch 3 (counts as 1 tr) at the beginning of each row, and work the last tr into the 2nd ch of the beg-ch before turning. Cont to work from the chart.
Rep chart rows until the block measures 15cm (6in) from the foundation chain. Fasten off yarn.

Repeat: 2 sts

ALTERNATE DOUBLE AND TREBLE CROCHET STITCHES

This stitch pattern produces a solid fabric with a subtle texture. Two stitches of differing heights can be substituted for the double and treble crochet shown here to produce a different but similar fabric. Taller stitches will produce a fabric with a lighter drape.

For a 15-cm (6-in) square block using a DK-weight yarn:
Foundation chain: ch 32.
Row 1: insert the hook into the 4th ch from the hook, work 1 dc; this completes the first 2 sts. Cont to work from the chart to the end of the row (29 sts). Row start ch (counts as 1 dc or 1 tr) at the beginning of each row, and work the last dc or tr into the bottom of the beg-ch before turning. Cont to work from the chart.
Rep chart rows until the block measures 15cm (6in) from the foundation chain. Fasten off yarn.

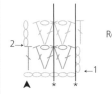

Repeat: 2 sts plus 1 st

BASKETWEAVE

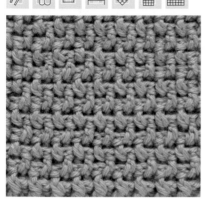

This stitch pattern produces a dense fabric that requires a lot of yarn for the area it covers, but it does provide a good framework when used in small sections. It is also possible to lighten the drape by substituting a taller stitch or interspersing with another stitch pattern.

For a 15-cm (6-in) square block using a DK-weight yarn:
Foundation chain: ch 30.
Row 1: yo, insert the hook into the 4th ch from the hook, work 1 tr; this completes the first 2 sts. Cont to work from the chart to the end of the row (28 sts).
Ch 3 (counts as 1 tr) at the beginning of each row, and work the last tr into the bottom of the beg-ch before turning. Cont to work from the chart.
Rep chart rows until the block measures 15cm (6in) from the foundation chain. Fasten off yarn.

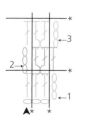

Repeat: 2 sts

RIB

This stitch pattern is similar to that of basketweave (left) but the post stitches are aligned on the same side of the fabric. This gives the fabric a better drape. This principle can be employed when combining other stitch patterns in the same block to the same effect.

For a 15-cm (6-in) square block using a DK-weight yarn:
Foundation chain: ch 30.
Row 1: yo, insert the hook into the 4th ch from the hook, work 1 tr; this completes the first 2 sts. Cont to work from the chart to the end of the row (28 sts).
Ch 3 (counts as 1 tr) at the beginning of each row and work the last tr into the bottom of the beg-ch before turning. Cont to work from the chart.
Rep chart rows until the block measures 15cm (6in) from the foundation chain. Fasten off yarn.

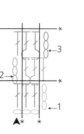

Repeat: 2 sts

TR IN THE FRONT LOOPS

This is a basic treble crochet stitch pattern with a treble crochet stitch worked into each stitch of the previous row, but each stitch is worked into the front loop only. This creates a rope-like line of loops. Because each new row of stitches is linked to the previous one by only one loop, the fabric has a lighter drape than a treble crochet fabric worked with the same hook through two loops.

Rep chart rows until the block measures 15cm (6in) from the foundation chain. Fasten off yarn.

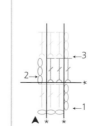

Repeat: 1 st

CALCULATING FOUNDATION CHAINS

To calculate the number of chains in a foundation chain when just a stitch repeat is given:

1 Using a gauge swatch of a similar stitch pattern, count the number of stitches required. Select the number nearest to this that meets the multiple of the stitch pattern to be worked, "x".

2 Check the pattern to see if the turning chain is counted as a stitch and what the first stitch is. Allow the following turning chains for each stitch:

double crochet
1 ch
half treble crochet
2 chs
treble crochet
3 chs
double treble
4 chs
triple treble
5 chs

3 If the turning chain does count as a stitch, subtract 1 ch from the repeat total "x" and add the number of turning chains that corresponds with the first stitch on row one.
    If the turning chain does not count as a stitch, subtract 1 ch and add the number of turning chains that corresponds with the first stitch on row one to "x".

14 TEXTURE IN BLANKETS

The fibre you use for knit or crochet will always create its own texture, but what you do with it in terms of stitch patterns can add even more.

For a knitter or crocheter the idea of raised stitches brings to mind the beautiful cables, twists, and bobbles of the knitted sweaters from the Aran Islands – but there are many other ways to raise the surface of the worked fabric. Even the simplest stitch or change of direction will add texture. Most ripple stitch patterns are an excellent way of giving an impression of texture and movement, yet still provide you with an easy, relaxing project.

RAISED STITCHES

From loopy stitches to bobbles, pleats, twists and cables, certain stitches can add texture to a blanket. In small amounts, all these elements can add interest as well as a contrasting tactile quality. Applying objects such as beads or knitted or crocheted flowers and leaves can also create raised areas.

△ **Elongated knit stitch bobble**
The elongated stitches were worked within a rib stitch pattern. As the rib contracts, so the form of the elongated stitches is exaggerated.

△ **Attach-later bobble**
This technique is a project saver. The bobble here has been used as a flower centre, but would be equally useful on a knitted or crocheted fabric that, once completed, looks as if it needs something extra.

△ **Beaded star**
Beads are a quick way of adding texture. Their weight can improve the drape of a fabric, and they can add sparkle – even when not in the form of a star.

△ **Elongated knit stitch**
This stitch can create a raised texture without the bulk of other raised stitch combinations.

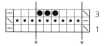

△ **Elongated knit stitch chart**
You can add this stitch to create a lighter texture if you place it in small groups in yarn that has very little stretch.

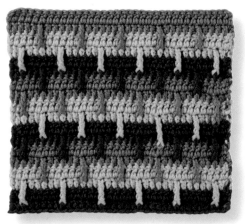

△ **Front-post stripes**
Even just a subtly raised stitch can bring texture to simple stripes.

△ No-turn bobble

When the blanket is a large, heavy, all-in-one this bobble is perfect. Extending the number of rows you work also creates a loop of fabric, which has enormous textural potential.

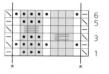

*k3, slip the sts back onto the left-hand needle, rep from * 3 more times.

△ No-turn bobble chart

This bobble is sometimes called an I-cord bobble and, like an I-cord, its appearance can be altered by how firm the yarn tension is at the start of each new row. The tension for this swatch was tight.

△ Loop stitch

In both knit and crochet, loop stitch is an excellent way to add texture and also to hide unsightly decreases such as those in this swatch. This swatch includes a fluffy yarn, which contrasts well with the acrylic yarn used for the rest of the swatch.

▷ An unusual use of yarn

The fibre used to make this strip consists of many odd lengths of yarn worked in one continuous chain, and then worked in treble crochet stitches into a space. It is an interesting way of using up impossibly small lengths of yarn, and has all the excitement of store-bought multi-coloured hand-dyed yarns when you work it.

▷ Working with fabric

Cutting denim into strips and then working it in crochet creates a dense texture that – although it provides very little of the "snuggle factor" – is durable, and makes an excellent edging if the blanket is to be supported on a flat surface. Different fabrics and different stitches would create varying effects. (Maybe all old clothes don't have to become dusters.) Worn fabric is perfect for this use; soft and pliable but strengthened by being stitched.

PINTUCKS

These pintucks are created by working to the base of the required pintuck, working twice the depth of the pintuck and then closing the pintuck by working each stitch together with its corresponding stitch at the base of the pintuck.

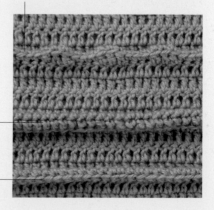

This pintuck is two rows deep and is created by working the first row in alternate pairs of double and treble crochet stitches. In the second row the matching stitch was worked to that in the first row, so the edge of the completed pintuck is wavy.

This pintuck is two treble crochet stitches deep. The second row of this pintuck fabric was worked through the front loops only so the edge of the completed pintuck is sharp.

This pintuck is two treble crochet stitches deep. The second row of this fabric was worked through the whole stitch so the edge of the completed pintuck is rounded.

CABLES AND TWISTS

Cable and twists have the benefit of adding an appearance of movement and flow in a blanket, but they can also limit the flexibility in a fabric.

Cables are a bulky texture that can restrict the drape of fabric by limiting its movement along its length and across its width. However, they also provide an attractive raised texture, and you can exploit the drape restrictions to work with the design intentions of your blanket.

KNITTED CABLES

Knitted cables consist of columns of stitches whose direction has been changed in relation to their neighbouring stitches. These columns are strengthened because they have the support of other stitches behind them that act as a scaffold. The main concern with knitted cables is how they look on the reverse. The traditional patterns often have a definite right and wrong side, with the wrong side not looking attractive at all.

Another concern is the drape of the fabric, which can become very heavy. This is because to make cables you must draw stitches together, and even a simple cable-four-forwards can require an increase of three stitches at its base to keep the width of the work constant. However, cables can usefully be used to influence the direction of drape a fabric has; it is more likely to drape along the lines of the cable. Remember that sometimes a relatively solid block is useful in the "skeleton" of a blanket to hold neighbouring blocks in shape. If it is towards the centre of the blanket its reverse is less likely to be revealed by turned-up edges.

△ **Pass stitch over**
This texture can sometimes be mistaken for a cable but it is not as bulky and is much quicker to execute.

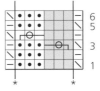

◁ **Pass stitch over chart**
The frequency of the passed-over stitches is easy to alter as is the direction in which they are passed.

k2, yo, k1, pass the first k st over the k, yo and k sts.

◁ **Cables and lace**
A garter stitch cable motif has been combined with a simple faggot lace to create a reversible cable pattern with light drape. Not all cable designs adapt well to garter stitch because the stitch height is less than stocking stitch and the stitches are stretched as they are moved in a cable sequence.

Slip 3sts onto the cable needle and hold at the back, k1, k2tog, yo, transfer the stitches from the cable needle back onto the left-hand needle, k2, k2tog.

◁ **Cables and lace chart**
This stitch pattern repeat is easily adjusted to create a different effect. This pattern was designed so that there were an odd number of cables evenly spaced across a 15-cm (6-in) swatch.

△ Chain action

The ribbed cable stitches make this pattern reversible. This principle can be adapted to other cable designs.

CROCHET CABLES

Crochet cables do bulk the fabric but they don't distort it so it is not necessary to recalculate the tension. However, to make for a more comfortable blanket, try using a larger hook to reduce the bulk and improve the drape (in which case you will need to calculate a new tension).

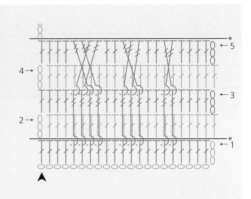

△ Crochet cable chart

A crochet cable, unlike a knitted cable, does not set a column of stitches off in a new direction, but instead misdirects the eye as to where the stitches have come from. This is done by means of front-post or raised stitches worked diagonally around stitches in previous rows.

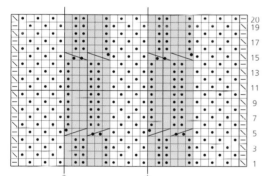

△ Chain action chart

The stitch repeat of this pattern is long but the seed-stitch spacing can be adjusted to suit your project's requirements.

Cable 6 back, slip the next 3 sts onto a cable needle and hold at the back of the work, k1, p2, transfer the stitches from the cable needle back onto the left-hand needle, k2, p1.

Cable 6 forward, slip the next 3 sts onto a cable needle and hold at the front of the work, p1, k2, transfer the stitches from the cable needle back onto the left-hand needle, p2, k1.

◁ Crossing cables

Lily Chin's solution for reversible cables is to cross knit stitches on a rib pattern so that the cross is hidden in the purl on the reverse side.

k2, and slip onto a cable needle holding it at the front of the work, slip 2 purl sts onto another cable needle and hold at the back, k2, from the left-hand needle, p2 from the cable needle at the back, k2 from the cable needle at the front.

▷ Crossing cables chart

The pattern is lost on a 1x1 rib, but a 3x3 rib is too dense. You can improve the drape by increasing the needle size, though the stitch pattern does start to lose definition.

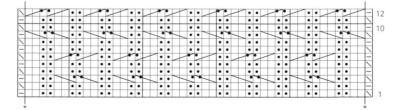

LACE IN BLANKETS

As well as being decorative, holes or spaces between stitches are an excellent way of improving the drape of a fabric.

Cheaper than bobbin lace, fine crochet and knitted lace have long been used in lightweight shawls and decorative linens. There are two types of lace: mesh patterns that tend to form a light background texture, and openwork, which is more decorative. Both rely on contrast with areas of solid or grouped stitches to be effective.

KNITTED LACE

Knitted lace is formed by yarnovers or by make-one increases that have been worked untwisted. Both these methods increase the number of stitches on the needle, so they need to be paired with decreases to keep the row counts correct. Where these decreases appear affects the finished fabric.

CROCHET LACE

In crochet lace, holes are formed by chains, missed stitches, and stitches of varying heights. The process is slightly more intuitive than in knitting and sometimes, in order to get the best finished result, counts must be adjusted to suit individual chain tension, which is prone to stretching and tightening.

△ Old Shale
Old Shale is a traditional Shetland Island design and is often worked on stocking stitch, so it is not identical on both sides.

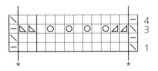

△ Old Shale chart
The yarnovers and decreases are grouped together, causing the fabric to expand where there are more stitches and contract where there are fewer stitches. This creates a wavy edge, which is difficult to contain within a block design but would work well in a blanket worked in one piece.

◁ Pineapple block
The basic idea of a pineapple design is a fan of tall stitches, worked on subsequent rows by smaller stitch units, which in turn are decreased by two with each row. The pineapple sequence here has been used to create a pineapple shape which in North American tradition symbolizes friendship and the welcoming of people to the heart of the home and hearth.

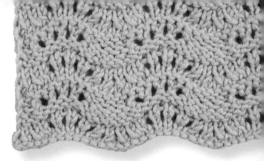

△ Adapted Old Shale
The Old Shale stitch pattern has been adapted to create a five-row repeat which means that row 1 of the repeat appears on alternate sides of the work.

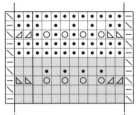

◁ Adapted Old Shale chart
The knit stitch into the yarnover on makes a slightly bigger hole than if the yarnover was purled.

△ Cat's paw
In this traditional design, the yarnovers and their respective decreases are placed close together and evenly, making it an ideal motif for a block design.

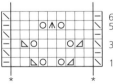

△ Cat's paw chart
The double decrease on row 5 is positioned so there are no yarnovers in the decreases on that row (which would reduce the size of the yarnovers). The double decrease also adds a neat finish to the block of stitches in the centre of the yarnovers. A single pattern repeat has been positioned within blocks of nine stitches by 12 rows of stocking and reverse stocking stitch to create a reversible design; with three rows before the start of the pattern repeat and three rows after the pattern repeat.

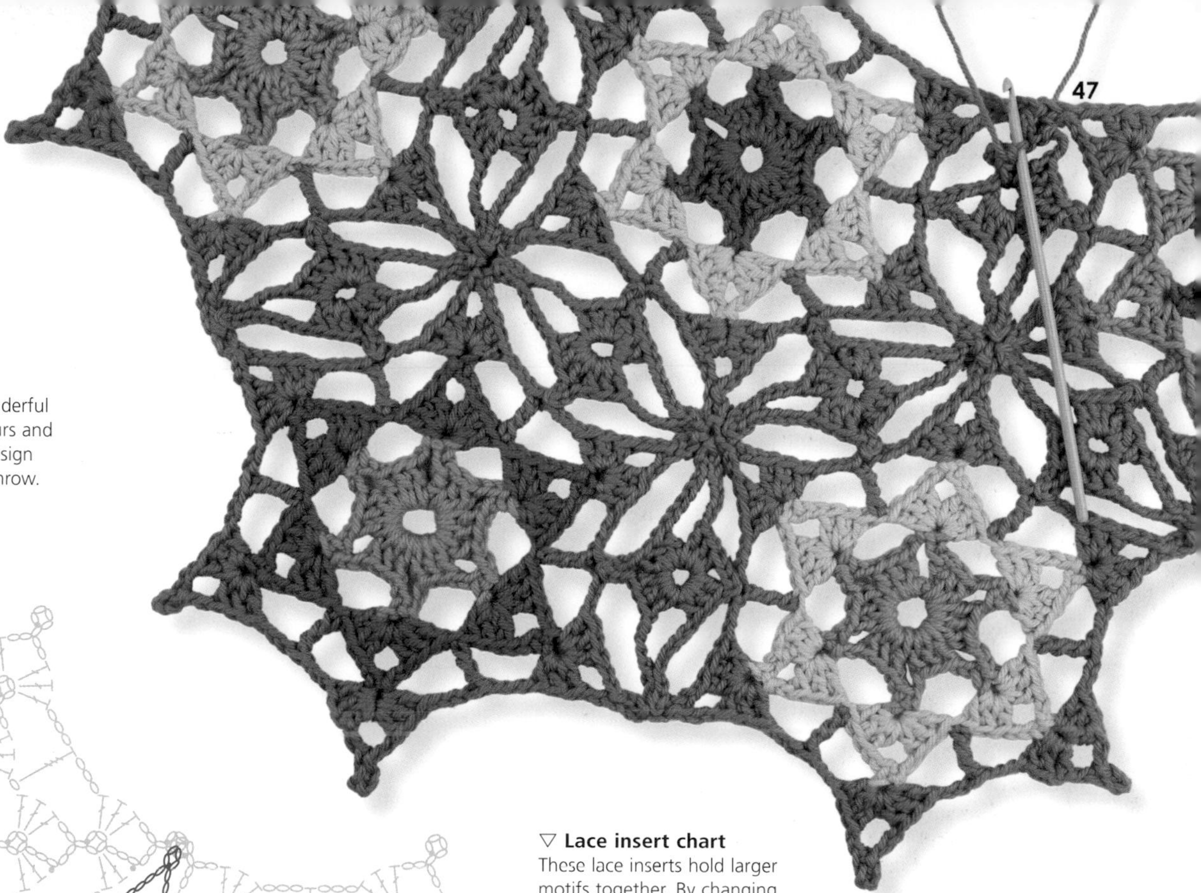

▷ Crochet star

Old tablecloth and doily patterns are a wonderful source of block ideas. Worked in four colours and DK-weight cotton, this traditional centre design has been adapted to create a lightweight throw. For the star pattern chart see page 27.

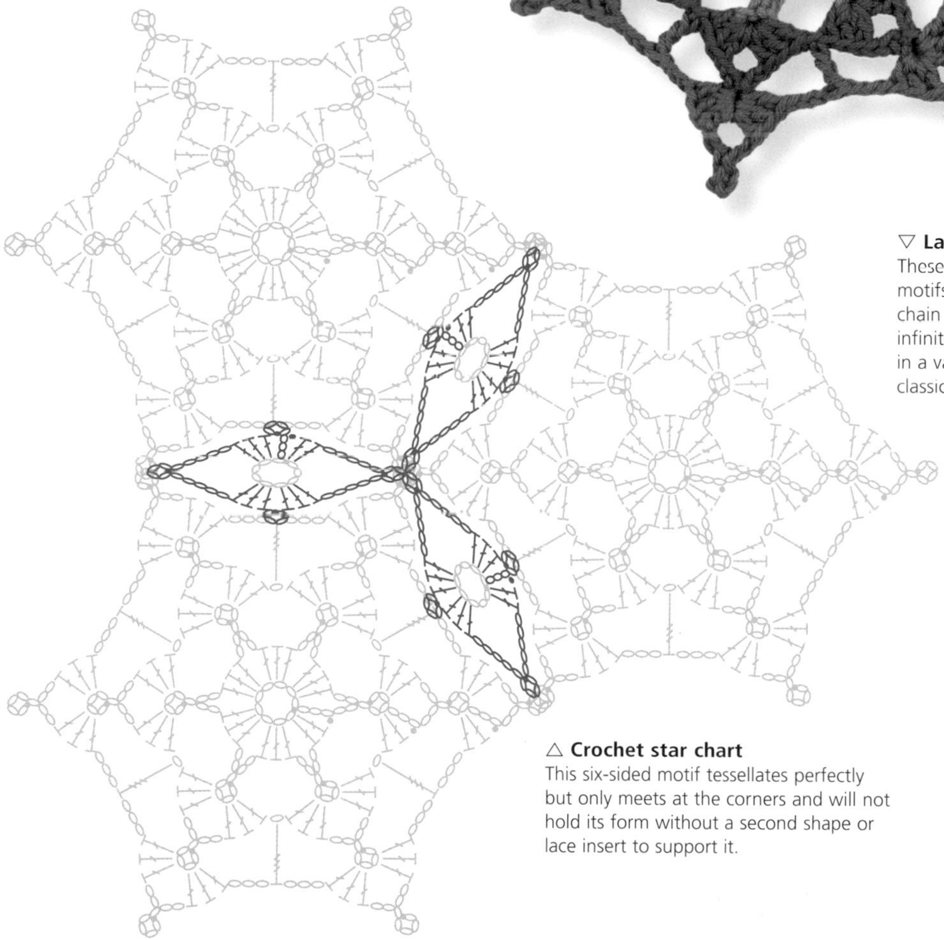

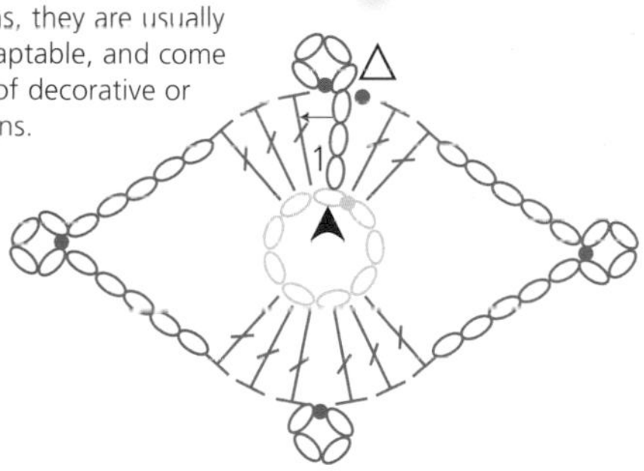

▽ Lace insert chart

These lace inserts hold larger motifs together. By changing chain lengths, they are usually infinitely adaptable, and come in a variety of decorative or classic designs.

△ Crochet star chart

This six-sided motif tessellates perfectly but only meets at the corners and will not hold its form without a second shape or lace insert to support it.

TIPS

More than any other texture, lace requires careful blocking for its full beauty to be revealed (see page 78).

If the lace is in the form of a block, try to position it in a blanket next to blocks that will help to maintain its shape.

KNITTED LACE BLOCKS

Lace is a classic knit texture that is lighter than a solid knitted fabric and is economical with yarn. But the really wonderful thing about lace is that holes are identical on both sides of the fabric!

Just as a lace pattern is about the contrast between the solid areas of stitches and the lighter texture of the yarnovers, in the larger context of a blanket, lacy blocks provide a contrast that can showcase other, more solid, blocks. There are hundreds of lacy stitch patterns published that you could use in a blanket, but lace blocks and patterns are not difficult to design for yourself. They can be used to create figurative or abstract images that can add to the visual story of a blanket, but care has to be taken to select designs that will fulfil the function of a blanket and not that of a shawl. To some extent this is avoided by the choice of a heavier yarn, but it is also important to know the limitations of the stitch pattern and only work at a scale that does not introduce gaping holes and result in a loss of form.

Although yarnovers and decreases are popular forms of lace knitting, there are other ways of creating holes in the fabric.

△ **Cable lace**
Yarnovers and decreases can be used to simulate cables and crosses, without the double thickness of fabric and unsightly reverse.

LADDERS

A fun way of making holes is to create ladders by dropping stitches. A dropped stitch is around three times as wide as a worked stitch, so the number of stitches across a given width is reduced. To contain a ladder within a block, you must make a stitch at the base of the ladder and then decrease again at the top. Ladders are particularly effective with variegated or space-dyed yarn as the horizontal strands form stripes of colour. These strands can also be embroidered or drawn into groups.

△ **Variegated ladders**
Often the first and last ladder of a run do not look as good, but these can be coaxed and blocked into submission by using a cable needle and easing or pulling the excess yarn into the adjacent stitches.

TIP

If the p2togtbl decreases don't appear to lie correctly, try the following: slip the next two stitches one at a time knitwise from the left-hand needle, insert the left-hand needle into the back of the slipped stitches from left to right, and purl the two stitches together.

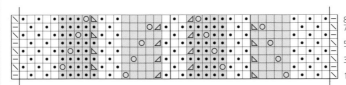

△ **Cable lace chart**
The decrease position is after the yarnover to allow for a smooth line of decreases and to prevent the need to work a decrease over a yarnover. The stitches involved in the cable effect panel are highlighted in blue.

△ **Charting a stitch run**
The double horizontal lines symbol for the ladder stitch is unusual in chart terms because it does not indicate an action but a placement. This stitch is simply worked in the usual way stated by the stitch pattern, but to keep track of which stitch is to be dropped, it is a good idea to work the stitch in the reverse stitch, purl on a knit row, and knit on a purl row.

ELONGATED STITCHES

Elongated stitches are created by inserting the right-hand needle into the next stitch on the left-hand needle as if to knit or purl, and wrapping the yarn more than once around the needle before drawing all the loops through and completing the stitch. On the next row, only one of the loops is worked and the rest are dropped off the left-hand needle. This produces a light fabric that grows quite quickly. If you worked every row as elongated stitches, the effect would be the same as working with over-large needles, but placing elongated stitches selectively produces waves or stripes. Elongated stitches work particularly well with textured yarn.

DOUBLE YARNOVERS

Double yarnovers can appear on a chart as two adjacent squares on a row with a yarnover symbol, or as a yarnover symbol with a "2" in the centre.

To create a double yarnover, work two yarnovers around the right needle before working along the row. On the next row, knit into the first yarnover and purl the second yarnover. This creates two stitches and a large hole. Two decreases will be required in order to keep the row count correct.

The slight bagginess created will not be apparent in close fabrics such as garter stitch, and makes this technique very useful for translating lace patterns from stocking stitch to garter stitch.

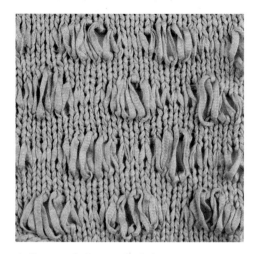

△ **Groups of elongated stitches**
If the stitches have too many wraps round the needle, or one area of the block has more elongated stitches and so the stitches cannot be stretched to their full depth when blocked, the strands will hang down over the fabric.

LACE ZIGZAG

This pattern has been worked on needles of differing sizes. Using a larger needle than usual to work the yarnovers creates a larger lace hole. The smaller size on the return row helps to define the rib element. For the pattern, see page 108.

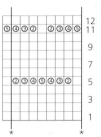

△ **Placement of elongated stitches**
The groups of elongated stitches are staggered across the fabric to enable it to be blocked to a square. If the groups of elongated stitches were to one side, the depth of the fabric at this point would be deeper and if any attempt were made to block it square, a lacy frill would be created. The circle symbol represents the number of times the yarn is wrapped around the needle, after the right-hand needle has been inserted into the stitch on the left-hand needle, before the stitch is completed. Only one of the wrapped stitches is worked on the following row; the rest are allowed to drop off the needle unworked.

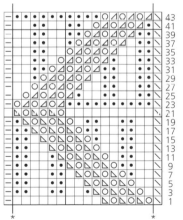

△ **Lace zigzag chart**
Only odd-numbered rows are shown on the chart, which are worked on a larger needle than those used for even-numbered rows.

DESIGNING LACE BLOCKS

Start by knitting a gauge swatch in the stitch pattern that is to form the background to the lace design and calculate how many stitches and rows make up the desired block size. Draw up a grid with one square indicating each stitch in the block and rough out the design using a yarnover symbol in a square to outline the shapes. For a very lacy effect or to achieve a certain line, yarnovers can be placed in adjacent squares – otherwise placing them every second square will work well.

In order to keep the stitch count correct, you must pair each yarnover with a decrease. The decrease can be next to the yarnover or a few stitches or rows away. Think carefully about which decrease to use. For instance, a right-slanting decrease such as knit-two-together or purl-two-together will slant to the right; if the yarnover is to the right of the decrease, the decrease will slant across the yarnover, making it appear smaller. The same is true for a left-slanting decrease and a yarnover to its immediate left. For a couple of rows after a yarnover, avoid putting a decrease immediately above it as the stitches below the decrease will be pulled slightly to form the stitch, and neighbouring stitches or yarnovers will appear smaller.

Experiment with the placement of the yarnovers and decreases until you reach a balance, then swatch the whole block and make any necessary adjustments. The block will then be ready to include in the blanket design.

Matching decreases

Some lace patterns may be worked on panels of stocking stitch, in which case it is useful to know the knit and purl equivalents of the most frequently used decreases. This will ensure the decreases will look the same, for instance on the knit side, whether worked in knit on the right side or in purl from the wrong side.

Type of decrease	knit	purl
Right-slanting	k2tog	p2tog
Left-slanting	ssk or sl1, k1, psso	p2togtbl
Double decrease	k3tog	p3tog
Double centre decrease	sl2tog, k1, psso	sl2tog, p3tog

Swatching makes good
It is a good idea to swatch several design variations to be sure that one will be right for the design. Yarnovers have been highlighted in red on the charts so their placement can easily be seen.

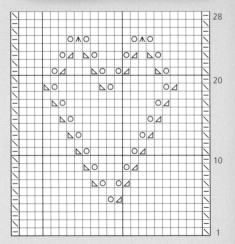

△ **Placing decreases**
A reliable trick to placing decreases is to put them towards the outside of the design and use the symbol shape that follows the outline of the yarnovers. The yarnovers and decreases are evenly distributed across the lace pattern in groups, creating a wave effect.

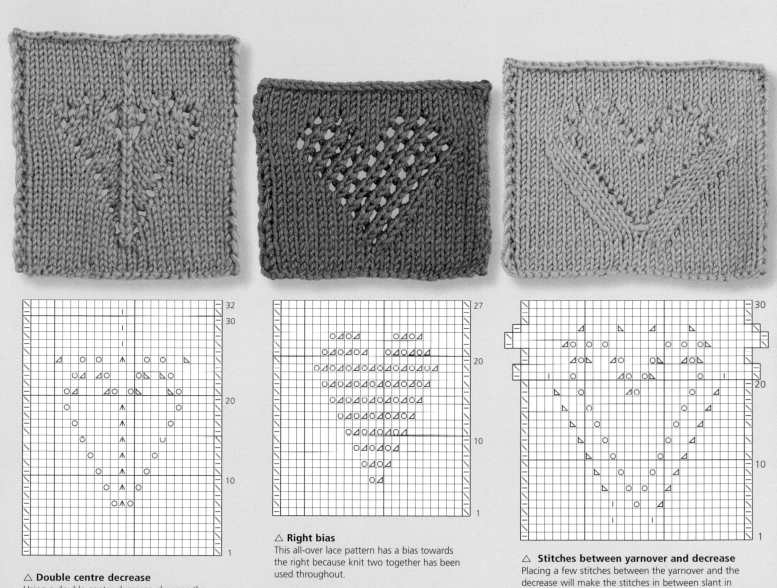

△ **Double centre decrease**
Using a double centre decrease changes the character of the motif as stitches either side of the decrease slant towards it.

△ **Right bias**
This all-over lace pattern has a bias towards the right because knit two together has been used throughout.

△ **Stitches between yarnover and decrease**
Placing a few stitches between the yarnover and the decrease will make the stitches in between slant in the same direction as the decrease.

CROCHET LACE

The intricate beauty of crochet lace bedspreads has adorned beds for centuries, and such beautiful objects have become treasured possessions.

There are two types of crochet lace. The first is a fabric made up of holes and solid areas created from strings of chain stitches and stitches that improve the drape of what could be a dense crochet fabric.

The second type of crochet bedspread is popular in Continental Europe. These bedspreads are not traditionally made from scraps of yarn but are worked in fine cotton or linen and in pale colours, and rely on the bed's underblanket showing through for colour. Often made to celebrate a wedding, or created by a young girl for her bottom drawer, they are created to display the maker's skill and imagination, rather than to produce a warm bedspread. They are used to cover the bed, often untouched, during the day and are folded up in the evening as the bed is prepared for the night. They can look uninviting and austere, or neat and proper, depending on your point of view. Work them in heavier yarns to create a more homey look, or their crispness and geometric form can be used to create a modern minimal look.

THE NEW OLD

It is fashionable to work the traditional patterns from Continental Europe in a chunky or bulky-weight yarn and use bright colours. A single, large motif can look very dramatic used as a bed throw in the centre of a large bed, but with limited weight and form, care has to be taken to position the throw neatly.

▷ **Designing crochet lace medallions**
It's not the design of the whole, but the design of its parts that is important when designing crochet medallions. Consider how many sides the medallion will have and that will become the number of its parts. This is a good basic centre rosette from which motifs of four and eight sides can easily be designed. For design inspiration, look at other medallions or lace patterns. Often only the chain lengths need to be adapted, or simply work as your hook takes you.

◁ **Four-sided medallion chart**
This is a basic design found in most crochet stitch directories. Experiment by adding popcorns – layers of stitches behind stitches – and different mesh stitches to change its appearance.

▽ Flower medallion chart

This is a very useful design because it can be easily adapted to fit most spaces.

△ Overlong chains

The chains in this design give it an organic rather than a geometric look. The drape is light but the design is less distinct. This look can be achieved with any medallion by making the chains a little long and using a slightly larger hook.

TIPS

Choose a hook with a tapered head. This makes inserting the hook into tight chains easier.

Lace charts and patterns will specify the number of chains from one section to another, but don't take this too literally. Chain stitch has very little to stabilize its structure and can vary enormously from hook to hook. Chain until the next stitch can be made and if the medallion won't lie flat, frog it.

19
FILET LACE

Filet is one of the easiest and quickest forms of crochet lace. Once the foundation row is established, it's just a matter of making a solid mesh or an open mesh. The mesh size can vary but the principles remain the same.

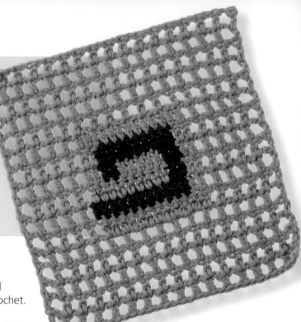

Filet crochet is a mesh of small blocks of stitches that are either worked, solid mesh, or skipped, open mesh. Designs are simple to chart on graph paper and, as the mesh is square, inspiration can easily be found in cross-stitch and knitting motifs. No wonder it is so popular.

However, the smallest mesh of a single-chain, treble crochet, and DK-weight yarn requires a grid of approximately 16 squares by 16 squares to create a 15cm (6in) square block. This is not a large number of mesh squares and it is not possible to get much detail into this grid. The solutions are either to use a finer yarn or to make larger blocks – perhaps double the size so they can still be matched with 15-cm (6-in) square blocks. Neither will necessarily be difficult as filet crochet works up quickly.

▽ Simple spiral
Even simple designs can look effective in filet crochet, but the fabric does lend itself to weaving or embroidery if more embellishment is needed (see Woven Crochet, page 58).

STARTING DESIGN

Consider careful distribution of open- and solid-mesh blocks when designing filet crochet. A row of solid-mesh blocks will bulge out slightly to the side as the double crochet stitch is slightly wider than the chain, but to a certain extent this can be eliminated in the blocking and finishing of the square.

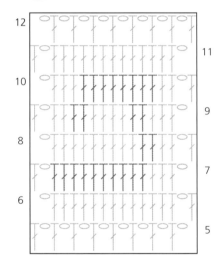

☐ Open mesh: ch 1, sk 1 sp or st, tr into the next st.

☐ Solid mesh: tr into the next sp or st, tr into the next st.

■ Solid mesh in a contrast colour.

◁ Mesh size
This design is worked on a single-mesh grid to maximize the amount of detail in a 15-cm (6-in) block.

△ Colour in filet crochet
It is possible to work colour into a filet design but it will be offset slightly because each unit of solid or open mesh starts with the stitch or stitches in the centre of a block and then ends with a stitch to form the side of the block.

◁ Two-colour filet
A second colour is more prominent if introduced to solid-mesh blocks, but a subtle effect can be obtained by working open-mesh blocks in a contrasting colour.

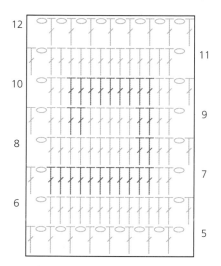

△ Adjusting colour blocks in filet crochet
The positions of the stitches in the contrast colour have been adjusted to create the straight lines of the design in the chart (top).

△ Radiating filet
As with all radiating motifs, this design is easy to adapt to different tensions and yarn weights.

FILET CROCHET IN THE ROUND

Filet crochet designs worked in the round are not as popular with publications as those worked back and forth, but they allow for a block to be worked in any yarn and stopped when it reaches the correct size. It produces a chain edge on all sides that makes the blocks easier to seam.

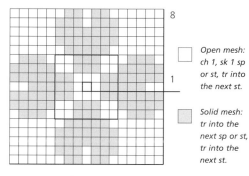

☐ Open mesh:
ch 1, sk 1 sp
or st, tr into
the next st.

▨ Solid mesh:
tr into the
next sp or st,
tr into the
next st.

△ Charting filet crochet in the round
The number of mesh blocks is an odd number with usually the centre nine mesh blocks open because they are difficult to fill convincingly.

△ Radiating filet chart
To adapt the chart, simply add or reduce the number of rounds either following the design set, or working a round or open-mesh block.

DIFFERENT MESH COMBINATIONS

Here are just a few of the various mesh proportions that can be used. In each case a formula has been given for the foundation chain. The additional chains at the end are the turning chain. Further chains may be required, depending on whether or not the first mesh is open.

Single-chain mesh is the smallest
Foundation chain = number of mesh squares x 2 + 3 chains

The fourth chain from the base of the hook will be the base of the first stitch, which will either be the first skipped stitch of an open mesh or the first treble crochet of a solid mesh. Add one chain if the first mesh block is open.

Open mesh: ch 1, sk 1 sp or st, tr into the next st.
Solid mesh: tr into the next sp or st, tr into the next st.

Double-chain mesh
Foundation chain = number of mesh squares x 3 + 3 chains

The fourth chain from the base of the hook will be the base of the first counted stitch, which will either be the first skipped stitch of an open mesh or the first treble crochet of a solid mesh. Add two chains if the first mesh block is open.

Open mesh: ch 2, sk sp or 2 sts, tr into the next st.
Solid mesh: tr twice into the next sp or once into each of the next 2 sts, tr into the next st.

Three-chain mesh with trebles
Foundation chain = number of mesh squares x 4 + 4 chains.

The fifth chain from the base of the hook will be the base of the first counted stitch, which will either be the first skipped stitch of an open mesh or the first double treble of a solid mesh. Add three chains if the first mesh block is open.

Open mesh: ch 3, sk sp or 3 sts, dtr into the next st.
Solid mesh: dtr 3 times into the next sp or once into each of the next 3 sts, dtr into the next st.

OTHER SHAPES IN THE ROUND

If filet crochet is worked in the round, you can create shapes other than squares – octagons for example. Work the first round as shown in the chart below, with one or two open-mesh blocks for every side of the shape. On the second round, work a corner, or a solid- or open-mesh sequence into the last completed stitch of the previous mesh, every one or two mesh blocks depending on the multiple of the first round. If you are designing your own motifs, there are two things to keep in mind: that the open-mesh blocks on the first round provide extra ease, which is often helpful; and try if possible to start each round along an edge rather than a corner.

▽ **Charting filet crochet octagons**
Each eighth is worked separately with a start chain or treble crochet at the beginning of each section. In every second round the start treble crochet and end treble crochet of a section are worked into the corner space. On alternate rounds, just the end treble crochet stitch of an eighth section is worked into the corner space.

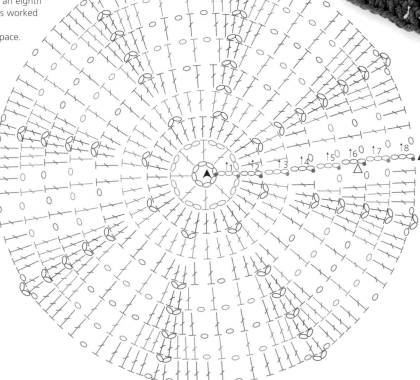

△ **Filet crochet octagon block**
This octagon block needs to be teamed with a square block to create a fabric with no large gaps. Striping the rounds allows for the use of odd scraps of yarn and emphasizes the shape when the blocks are pieced, and the edges are no longer so apparent.

DIAGONALLY FILLED MESH ON A SINGLE-CHAIN MESH

One way of adding detail is to work a half mesh. There are several ways of doing this. A double-chain mesh or three-chain mesh can have one treble crochet or double treble worked in a block space rather than two or three, creating a shaded effect, or a mesh can have a series of stitches that diagonally fill the box.

Half mesh, bottom left: ch 1, yo, insert the hook into the tr st, yo, draw yarn through 2 loops on the hook, insert the hook into next tr st, yo, draw yarn through, yo draw yarn through 1 loop on the hook, yo, draw the yarn through all the loops on the hook.

Half mesh, bottom right: insert the hook into the base of the last tr worked, yo, draw yarn through, yo draw yarn through 1 loop on the hook, yo, sk 1 st, insert the hook into the next tr st, yo, draw yarn through 2 loops on the hook, yo, draw the yarn through all the loops on the hook, ch 1.

Half mesh, top left: sk next sp or st, 2tr into the next tr st.

Half mesh, top right: tr into the base of the last tr worked, sk next sp or st, tr into the next tr st.

FILET AND FIBRES

Filet designs can be worked in any fibre, but the crisper the appearance of the fibre the crisper the image. In fact, filet crochet lends itself to cotton yarns – its open nature means that the finished blanket will not suffer from the weight of the cotton. Another yarn characteristic to look for is an even colour. Variegated yarns or self-striping yarns can be distracting in filet motifs, and it can take the eye a while to decipher the design.

The Lurex yarn has a distracting sparkle, but the design should still be quite clear.

The mercerized cotton has particularly good stitch – and therefore mesh – definition.

The more fluffy nature of the wool yarn makes the open-mesh blocks less distinct than that of the smooth cotton.

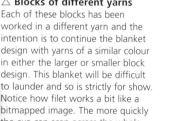

△ **Blocks of different yarns**
Each of these blocks has been worked in a different yarn and the intention is to continue the blanket design with yarns of a similar colour in either the larger or smaller block design. This blanket will be difficult to launder and so is strictly for show. Notice how filet works a bit like a bitmapped image. The more quickly the eye can scan across the whole block, the easier it will be to recognize the design.

▽ **Fair Isle filet crochet charts**
These block designs are based on a Fair Isle knitting design and they have not been adapted for the proportions of filet crochet.

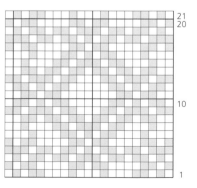

EMBROIDERY

Simple embroidery adds a personal touch to your work. You can add flowers, animals, birds, a name or a date; whatever you like.

DUPLICATE STITCH ON STOCKING KNITTING

Duplicate stitch, as its name suggests, exactly copies the structure of a knitted stitch. It is best used for outline designs like this flower, because large areas of duplicate stitch tend to thicken the knitted fabric, making it less flexible.

Always use a blunt-tipped tapestry needle to avoid splitting the knitted stitches. Follow the embroidery guidelines below.

Try to match the embroidery to the size of the knitted stitches. The embroidered design looks as if it has been knitted in.

FREESTYLE EMBROIDERY

Freestyle embroidery may be worked across the surface of knitting or crochet. A plain knit or crochet background is best; the examples below are shown on stocking stitch knitting. Follow the embroidery guidelines (see below and right), using a sharp needle with a large eye, such as a darning needle.

▽ **Backstitch**
Use this stitch for outlines and fine lines.

Bring the needle through the back of the work. From the front and in one motion, take the needle through to the back a short distance along to the right, then draw back through the work to the front the same distance along to the left from the beginning of the stitch. Continue from right to left by inserting the needle through from front to back at the point where the last stitch emerged.

▽ **Stem stitch**
This stitch is useful for creating curved lines (such as flower stems) and outlines.

Bring the needle through from the back of the work, then insert it through the piece from front to back a short distance to the right at a slight angle. The distance will depend on how large you wish the stitch to be.

Duplicate stitch

1 Bring the needle out at the base of the knitted stitch to be duplicated. Pass the needle behind the two "legs" of the stitch above. Pull through.

2 Insert the needle again at the base of the same knitted stitch, where it first emerged, and bring it out at the base of the next knitted stitch to be duplicated. Here, a line of duplicate stitch is being worked from right to left. Repeat as required, counting the stitches carefully.

▽ Chain stitch

This stitch makes a bold line that may be straight or curved. Chain stitch also mimics the elasticity of the background knitting.

Bring the needle through from the back. * In one motion, take the yarn through from front to back at the point where the first yarn came through to the front, to create a loop. Bring the needle back through to the front a short distance along to the left and through the centre of the loop. Tighten and repeat from *.

At the end of the line, hold down the last chain loop with a small stitch over the loop, as shown for lazy daisy stitch, below.

▽ French knot

French knots are useful for flower centres, and can also be used to add little dots of colour wherever required.

Bring the needle through where required and wrap the yarn twice around the needle. Holding the yarn taut, insert the needle one knitted strand away from where it emerged. (Don't insert the needle in exactly the same place, or the knot will disappear through to the back of the knitting.) Pull through gently.

▽ Blanket stitch

This stitch may be worked along an edge, as shown, to stengthen it and reduce curling. Alternatively, it may be worked flat as part of an embroidered design.

Working from left to right, bring the needle through the piece from the back, approximately one row in from the edge of the fabric. From the front, thread the needle through to the back, one stitch to the right, point the needle upwards, catch the loop of yarn around it and pull through.

▽ Lazy daisy stitch

Single chain stitches may be arranged to form little flowers. Hold down the loop of each chain with a small stitch.

Make a chain stitch as described above, but instead of making a running sequence of stitches, sew a small stitch over the top of the chain to hold the loop in place. Repeat this in the formation of a small flower, each chain representing one petal.

GENERAL EMBROIDERY GUIDELINES

- Choose smooth yarns for embroidery, of the same fibre as the knitting or crochet.
- Cut lengths of embroidery yarn no longer than 60cm (24in).
- Begin by passing the needle through to the back of the work, leaving a 10-cm (4-in) tail on the surface. Then bring the needle up where the first stitch is required.
- Do not pull stitches too tightly, or the knitting will be distorted.
- Do not pass the embroidery yarn behind more than two or three stitches between embroidered areas — fasten off and start again.
- When complete, pull all the tails through to the back and run them in along the back of matching embroidery stitches where they won't show.

▽ Freestyle embroidery on crochet

Embroidery stitches need a fairly plain background to show to their best advantage, and even the plainest crochet stitch has more texture than stocking stitch knitting. So for embroidery on crochet, choose bold stitches and bright colours.

21 WOVEN CROCHET

Simple crochet stitches may be used as a basis for woven crochet. After making a piece of crochet fabric in a simple stitch with regular holes, contrasting yarns are woven through the holes using a tapestry needle. Woven crochet is ideal for blankets and throws because the weaving process makes the crochet background more stable. For an all-in-one blanket design, it's easy to use the weaving tails to make a fringe.

SUITABLE WEAVING YARNS

Choose a strong yarn that will not easily fray, especially when weaving large areas, otherwise the action of pulling the yarn through all the holes may spoil its appearance, weaken it or even cause it to break. Several strands of fine yarn may be used together to suit the size of the crochet holes.

Contrasting colours, of course, show off the technique well, but you could also try contrasting textures – for example, try weaving fluffy yarns through smooth cotton crochet, or add sparkle to wool crochet with yarns containing Lurex. You can weave with narrow ribbon, too.

TO WORK THE WEAVING

1 Weave all the rows of holes in the same way. Measure the length of the first row of holes to be woven and add about 25cm (10in) to this measurement. Cut two or more strands of contrasting yarn to this length and thread them into a blunt-tipped tapestry needle. Pass the needle through the crochet, up and down, along a row of holes. Leave a tail of about 12.5cm (5in) at each edge of the crochet.

2 When all the weaving is complete, gently stretch the crochet in both directions to make sure that none of the weaving is too tight. The weaving yarn tails may be enclosed within a firm crochet edging, such as double crochet edging, or used to make fringes.

For each tail, thread one strand (or half the strands, if there are several) into the tapestry needle, pass the needle around the edge of the crochet and back up again through the first hole. Then tie both strands (or all the strands) with an overhand knot. When all the tails have been fringed, trim them to an equal length.

VARIATIONS

Various patterns can be built up using woven crochet.

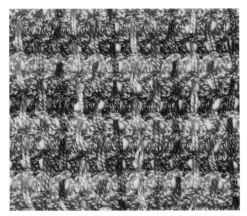

Worked in cotton yarns, this pattern is woven on a background of small mesh, worked in single-row stripes of three colours. The rows of holes are woven with the same three colours, used in turn, beginning the first woven line over the first bar, and the second woven line under the first bar, and so on alternately across the work.

OPENWORK MESH

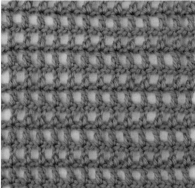

This stitch is very easy to work and makes a good introduction to this type of stitch for the beginner. It also makes a good background stitch for surface crochet.

For a 15-cm (6-in) square block using a DK-weight yarn:
Foundation chain: ch 34.
Foundation row: (RS) 1 tr into 6th ch from hook, * ch 1 , sk next ch, 1 tr into next ch; rep from * to end, turn.
  ow 1: ch 4 (counts as 1 tr, ch 1), * 1 tr into next tr, ch 1; rep from * to end, working last dc into 2nd of beg skipped ch 5, turn.
  ow 2: ch 4 (counts as 1 tr, ch 1), * 1 tr into next tr, ch 1; rep from * to end, working last tr into 3rd of ch 3, turn.
Rep row 2 for length required.
Fasten off.

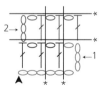

Repeat: 2 sts plus 3 sts

PLAIN TRELLIS

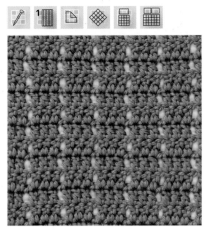

Another easy-to-work stitch, which is lovely when used to make a lightweight wrap, scarf or stole. It's reversible, so you can choose which side you prefer as the right side.

For a 15-cm (6-in) square block using a DK-weight yarn:
Foundation chain: ch 32.
Foundation row: 1 dc into 6th ch from hook, * ch 5, sk ch 3, 1 dc into next ch; rep from * to end, turn.
  ow 1: * Ch 5, 1 dc into next ch 5 sp; rep from * to end, turn.
Rep row 1 for length required.
Fasten off.

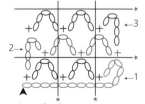

Repeat: 4 sts plus 2 sts

VERTICAL OPEN STRIPE

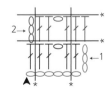

Other suitable stitches include patterns with mesh holes arranged in vertical or horizontal rows, such as this vertical open stripe.

For a 15-cm (6-in) square block using a DK-weight yarn:
Foundation chain: ch 33.
  ow 1: 1 tr in 4th ch from hook, 1 tr in next ch, *ch 1, skip 1 ch, 1 tr in each of next 3 ch,* repeat from * to * to end.
  ow 2: ch 3, skip first tr, 1 tr in next tr, *1 tr in next tr, ch 1, skip 1 ch, 1 tr in each of next 2 tr, *repeat from * to *, ending with 1 tr in 3rd of 3 ch.
Repeat row 2.
Fasten off.

Repeat: 4 sts plus 5 sts

22 BEAD KNITTING

Beads add sparkle and a touch of colour to knitted throws. However, they should be considered as decorative rather than practical. Choose the right beads for your project, thread them onto the knitting yarn as described below, then use the method given to knit beads in as your work proceeds.

CHOOSING BEADS

The holes in the beads must be large enough to slip easily along the yarn you are using.

Beads may be made of plastic, glass, wood, metal or ceramic. Plastic and wooden beads are generally lightweight, whereas glass, metal and ceramic beads may be heavier and add considerably to the weight of your project.

For washability, choose plastic beads; other materials may not withstand frequent washing.

PLACING A BEAD IN FRONT OF A SLIP STITCH

Placing beads with a slip stitch is done using garter stitch or stocking stitch on the right side of the work. Beads can be placed every alternate stitch and every other row. The bead falls directly in front of the slipped stitch.

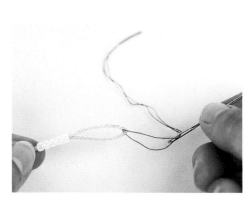

THREADING BEADS ONTO YARN

In most cases it is not possible to thread the knitting yarn directly through the bead. To do this, thread the needle using both ends of a piece of sewing thread. Place the yarn through the loop of thread, then pass the beads over the eye of the needle and onto both threads.

1 Work to where the bead is required. Slide the bead up the yarn. Bring the yarn forwards between the needles with the bead to the front and slip the next stitch purlwise.

2 Keep the bead as close to the knitting as possible, holding it in front of the slipped stitch with a finger or thumb if necessary, then take the yarn back between the needles, leaving the bead in front. Knit the next stitch firmly.

ALTERNATE BEADS

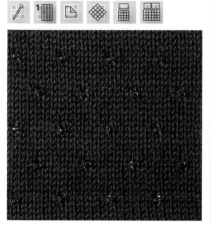

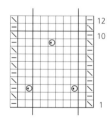

Simple arrangements of beads are easy to add to stocking stitch.

Before starting to knit, thread all the beads required onto the yarn. For pattern row 3 you will need 1 bead for every 6 sts, plus 1; and for pattern row 9, 1 bead for every 6 sts.

For a 15-cm (6-in) square block using DK-weight yarn:
Cast on 35 sts plus the selvedge sts using the thumb method.
Cont to work from the chart.
Rep rows until the block measures 15cm (6in) from the cast-on edge.
Cast off.

Repeat: 6 sts plus 3sts plus selvedge sts

BEAD TREE

Beads can be arranged to form simple motifs, like this tree:

Before starting to knit, thread all the beads required onto the yarn. Each tree motif requires 31 beads.

For a 6-in (15-cm) square block using DK-weight yarn:
Cast on 35 sts plus the selvedge sts using the thumb method.
Work 10 rows in rev st st.
To centre the chart motif, k6, pm, cont to work from the chart, pm k6.
Cont to work from the chart working the sts either side in rev st st.
Work in rev st st until the block measures 15cm (6in) from the cast-on edge.
Cast off.

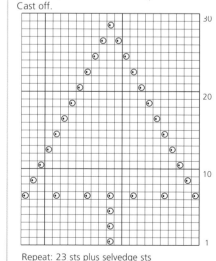

Repeat: 23 sts plus selvedge sts

TEXTURED PATCHWORK

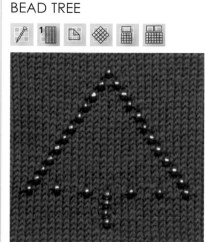

Beads can also be added to more complex stitch patterns, like this cable design:

Before starting to knit, thread all the beads required onto the yarn. Every beaded square of the pattern requires 8 beads.

For a 15-cm (6-in) square block using DK-weight yarn:
Cast on 32 sts plus the selvedge sts using the thumb method.
Cont to work from the chart.
Rep rows until the block measures 15cm (6in) from the cast-on edge.
Cast off.

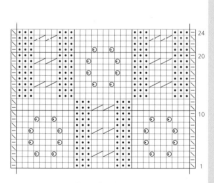

Repeat: 30 sts plus selvedge sts

TIPS

Avoid using beads on blankets for babies or young children because if the beads work loose, they can pose a choking hazard.

Always test the washing process on a sample knitted with the same beads; some need checking for colour-fastness.

BEAD CROCHET

Beads can be added to crochet as the work proceeds, giving a touch of sparkle and glamour. Beads added in this way are more secure than beads sewn on after the work is complete. Choose beads to suit your project following the same guidelines given for bead knitting on page 62. Then follow the crochet method described below.

BEADING ON DOUBLE CROCHET

Beads are applied while working wrong side rows and will then appear on the right side of the work. Thread the beads onto the yarn in the same way as for bead knitting (see page 62).

1 Work to the position of the first bead on a wrong side row. Slide the bead down the yarn until it rests snugly against the right side of your work.

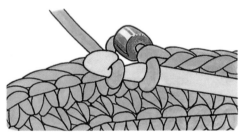

2 Keeping the bead in position, insert the hook in the next stitch and draw yarn through so there are two loops on the hook.

3 Wrap the yarn over the hook again and draw it through to complete the stitch. Continue adding beads in the same way across the row, following the pattern instructions.

DOUBLE CROCHET WITH BEADS

Special abbreviation: bdc = bead on double crochet, as described left.

Begin by threading beads onto yarn: on every 4th row, you need 1 bead for every 4 sts.

Requires a multiple of 4 sts, plus 1.

Work at least 2 or 3 rows of double crochet.

Row 1 (wrong side row): 1 ch, skip first dc, 1 dc in next dc, *1 bdc in next dc, 1 dc in each of next 3 dc, repeat from *, ending 1 dc in last dc, 1 dc in 1 ch, turn.

Row 2: 1 ch, skip first dc, 1 dc in each st ending 1 dc in 1 ch, turn.

Rows 3 and 4: as row 2. Repeat rows 1 to 4.

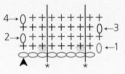

BEADING ON OTHER CROCHET STITCHES

When adding beads to stitches other than double crochet, proceed as follows:
Thread the required beads onto the yarn, as described on page 62.

Work the stitch up to the last "yarn round hook, pull through". Slide the bead along the yarn until it rests against the work. Catch the yarn beyond the bead and pull the yarn through the last loop(s) on the hook, thus completing the stitch.

As for double crochet, beads are applied on wrong side rows, and appear on the right side of the work.

TREBLE CROCHET WITH ALTERNATE BEADS

Special abbreviation: btr = bead on treble crochet: yrh, insert hook as directed, yrh, pull through 2 loops, slide bead along yarn close to work, yrh (catching yarn beyond bead), pull through both loops on hook.
Begin by threading beads onto yarn: on row 1, you need 1 bead for every 6 sts, minus 1; on pattern row 3, 1 bead for every 6 sts.
Requires a multiple of 6 sts, plus 1.
Work at least 1 row of trebles.
Row 1 (wrong side row): 3 ch, skip first tr, 1 tr in each of next 5 tr, *1 btr in next tr, 1 tr in each of next 5 tr, repeat from **, ending 1 tr in each of last 5 tr, 1 tr in 3rd of 3 ch, turn.
Row 2: 3 ch, skip first tr, 1 tr in each st ending 1 tr in 3rd of 3 ch, turn.
Row 3: 3 ch, skip first tr, 1 tr in each of next 2 tr, *1 bdc in next tr, 1 tr in each of the next 5 tr, repeat from * to last 4 sts, 1 btr in next tr, 1 tr in each of last 2 tr, 1 tr in 3rd of 3 ch, turn.
Row 4: as row 2
Repeat rows 1 to 4.

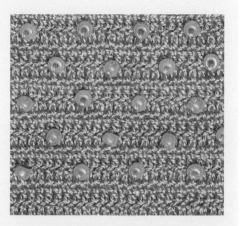

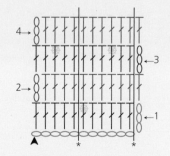

BEADED EDGINGS

Beads make a delightful addition to crochet edgings, too. The extra weight of a beaded edging can help a blanket or throw to drape well and hang in smooth folds.

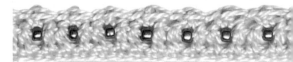

△ **Beaded waves**
Thread the beads onto the yarn: 1 bead for every 2 sts.
Make a foundation chain of the required length, or work row 1 directly into the item to be trimmed with right side facing (odd number of stitches).
Row 1: 1 ch, 1 tr into each st to end, turn.
Row 2: 3 ch, *bring down a bead to work into next dtr, 1 dtr, rep from * to end.
Row 3: 1 ch, *1 htr, 1 tr, rep from * to end.
Fasten off.

△ **Bead loops**
Thread beads onto yarn: 8 beads per loop are shown here, and 1 loop for every 3 sts. Make a foundation chain of the required length, or work row 1 directly into the item to be trimmed with the right side facing (multiple of 3 sts + 1).
Row 1: 1 ch, 1 tr in each ch to end, turn.
Row 2: as row 1.
Row 3: as row 1.
Row 4: 1 ch, *2 tr, bring down 8 beads, tr in next st, rep from * to end, turn.
Row 5: as row 1. Fasten off.

24 APPLIQUÉ

Appliqué motifs are worked separately, then sewn onto a knitted or crochet background. You can add motifs to certain blocks of a blanket in a regular arrangement, or scatter the motifs wherever you like for a more random appearance.

NEEDLE FELTING

A felting needle tool and mat can be used to apply yarn to knitting or crochet, to make areas of solid colour or outline designs. When worked correctly, a fuzzy version of the design shows through on the wrong side, so this technique is suitable for a reversible blanket.

PATCHES

Small knitted or crocheted patches such as squares, triangles and diamonds may be attached by sewing all around the edges with blanket stitch (see page 59) or other embroidery stitches.

△ **Buttoned patch**
This diagonally knitted square patch in garter stitch is attached with four buttons to a stocking stitch background.

△ **Felting tool**
As you punch with the tool, five barbed needles interlace the wool fibres so the design is permanently fixed in place. Woollen yarns give the best results, punched onto a background of knitting, as shown, or crochet. Follow the instructions supplied with the kit.

KNITTED APPLIQUÉ MOTIFS

Below are some ideas for knitted appliqué motifs that can be applied in clusters or as repeating designs across the work.

SINGLE PETAL

Single petals and leaves may be knitted and stitched in place to make a flower. Attach them to a knitting or crochet background by sewing around the outside edges.

Cast on 3 sts.
Row 1 (wrong side row): p.
Row 2: k1, m1 tbl, k1, m1 tbl, k1. 5 sts.
Row 3: p.
Row 4: k2, m1 tbl, k1, m1 tbl, k2. 7 sts.
Row 5: p.
Row 6: p3, m1 tbl, k1, m1 tbl, k3. 9 sts.
Rows 7–11: work in stocking stitch, beg and ending p row.
Row 12: p3, s2togk, k3. 7 sts.
Row 13: p.
Row 14: k2, s2togk, k2. 5 sts.
Row 15: p.
Row 16: k1, s2togk, k1. 3 sts.
Row 17: p.
Row 18: s2togk. Fasten off.

SINGLE LEAF

Work as for the single petal above, using the yo increase instead of m1 tbl.

LACY FLOWER

Knit this five-petal flower from the centre to the outside edge. The size of the finished flower will depend on the yarn and type of needles you use.

Using recommended needle size, cast on 13 sts.
Row 1 (wrong side row): p.
Row 2: k twice in each st. 26 sts.
Row 3: p.
Row 4: k1, * k2, yo twice, k2, *repeat from * to * to last st, k1. 38 sts.
Row 5: p1, * p2, p into front of first yo and back of second yo, p2, * repeat from * to * to last st, p1.
Row 6: k1, * (k1, insert needle into next hole, yrn, pull through a loop) 5 times in same hole, k1, * repeat from * to * to last st, k1. Do not pull the loops too tightly. 68 sts.
Row 7: p.
Cast off loosely.
Join side edges. Leave the centre open or gather it up to close the hole. Sew the centre of the flower where required or sew down all around the outside edge.

CROCHET APPLIQUÉ MOTIFS

Small crochet motifs are quick and simple to make and may be stitched in place wherever you want them.

IRISH LEAF

Note: work into back loop only on each repeat of row 2. Make 11 ch.
Row 1: working into one loop only along first side of ch, 1 tr into 2nd ch from hook, 1 tr in each of next 8 ch, 3 tr in last ch, working in one loop only along other side of foundation ch, 1 tr in each of next 7 ch, turn.
Row 2: working in back loop only, 1 ch, 1 tr in first tr, 1 tr in each of next 7 tr, 3 tr in next tr, 1 tr in each of next 7 tr, turn. Rep row 2 as many times as desired. Fasten off.

CLOVER

Special abbreviation: ttr3tog = work one ttr into each of same place as last st and the next 2 tr until 1 loop of each remains on hook, yo and through all 4 loops on hook. Make 5 ch, sl st into first ch to form a ring.
Round 1: 1 ch, 10 tr into ring, sl st into first tr.
Round 2: 1 ch, 1 tr into first dtr, *4 ch, ttr3tog, 4 ch, 1 tr in same place as last st, 1 tr in next tr, rep from * twice.
Make stalk: 7 ch (or number required), turn, 1 tr in 2nd ch from hook, 1 tr in each ch, sl st in first tr on round. Fasten off.

BOBBLES

Small bobbles can be knitted separately and sewn onto a knitted or crochet background.

Using recommended needle size, cast on 5 sts.
Work 7 rows stocking stitch, ending p row.
Pass the 1st, 2nd, 3rd, and 4th sts over the 5th st, and off the needle. Cut the yarn leaving an 20-cm (8-in) tail and pull through. Thread the tail onto a tapestry needle and run the needle in and out, all around the edge of the piece. Push the wrong side to the inside, adding a pinch of toy stuffing, if required. Gather tightly and sew the bobble in place.

Eleven bobbles make up this bunch of grapes. The stalk is embroidered in chain stitch (see page 59).

SILHOUETTE FLOWER

Make 20 ch, sl st in first ch to form a ring.
Round 1: 1 ch, 38 tr in ring, sl st in first tr.
Round 2: *9 ch, miss 6 tr, sl st in next tr, rep from * 4 times, sl st in each of next 3 tr.
Round 3: 2 tr in each 9-ch loop, 1 tr in each of next 3 sl sts, sl st to first tr.
Round 4: 3 ch, 1 dtr in each tr, sl st in first tr of round.
Make stem: 14 ch, 1 tr in 3rd ch from hook, 1 tr in each of next 11 ch. Fasten off.

WORKING WITH MODULAR ELEMENTS

A block is the most common modular element. Learning new ways of creating and using blocks can make you reconsider the possibilities they offer.

One-piece blankets are a delight to work when you are at home comfortably sat down, but they become heavy and cumbersome as completion draws close. The solution is to split a project into sections. These sections, or modular elements, can be square blocks, regular-shaped motifs or medallions, strips or larger panels.

DESIGNING MODULAR ELEMENTS

Block blankets define modular elements that must be created and pieced together. But this is not the case with all blankets. In their simplest terms, modular blankets may consist of the centre fabric and the edging; more complex blankets contain modular elements such as centre panels, side panels, blocks, top and bottom trimmings and edgings. A useful way to think about modular elements is to look for blocks of colour or yarn or stitch patterns. The same rationale can be extended to block construction too.

△ **Texture-striped block**
Alternate sides of this motif are worked in front-post and back-post stitches for four rounds. A second side is worked in the same stitch as the last, then alternate post stitches are worked along each edge again.

PROVISIONAL CAST-ON

A provisional cast-on allows the stitches of a cast-on to remain exposed and then knitted in another direction for a border or edging, or worked in Kitchener stitch, or grafted onto another set of stitches to create an apparently seamless join between two blanket modules. This cast-on can also be left unpicked to create a chain-like edge that can be seamed like a crochet edge. Choose a hook one size bigger than the recommended needle size or the one being used. (This is easier to ascertain if the metric system is used.)

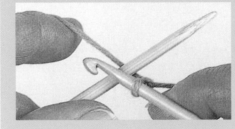

1 Using a contrasting cotton yarn, make a slip knot and insert the crochet hook through the loop. Then, holding the crochet hook in the left hand and the knitting needle in the right hand, take the yarn behind the knitting needle.

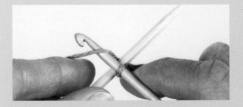

2 Wrap the yarn over the hook and draw the loop through the loop on the hook. Take the yarn back behind the needle and repeat the sequence.

3 Repeat Steps 1 and 2 until the required number of stitches are on the needle. Work a few chains without taking the yarn back behind the needle, then extend the last loop so that it will not unravel, and cut the waste yarn. Continue to work these stitch loops in the yarn and stitch pattern planned.

4 To pick up the stitch loops along the cast-on edge, pull the tail of the waste yarn at the end of the last cast-on loop and draw the extended loop through the last chains until it reaches the knitted fabric. Continue to pull the yarn tail, using a needle to pick up the loops along the base of the fabric as the crochet chain unravels. If the loops are hard to see insert the needle through them as the waste yarn loop pulls through it.

If the cast-on is to be used to create a crochet chain edge, repeat steps 1 and 2 until the number of stitches is one less than required, then transfer the loop on the crochet hook onto the needle to form the last stitch.

◁ **Modular blocks**

The easiest way to create a circle design in crochet is to work from the centre and increase on every round until the desired size is reached. If the circle is to be part of a block design then one solution is to work a crochet or knit mitred block, see page 73, and when the mitred block row length is double the diameter of the circle, join the two modules together.

▽ **No-pattern blocks**

This method does not rely on tension to create a block of the correct size. Start with a slip knot and work an increase, then, for every following row, knit to the last stitch and work an increase into the last stitch. Continue in the pattern set until the edges of the triangle created are equal to those of the block required, then, for every following row, knit until two stitches remain and knit these two stitches together. Repeat this row until one stitch remains, then fasten off. This technique works on the principle that one stitch over two rows of garter stitch occupies a square shape, its depth is equal to its width.

△ **Modular edgings**

Stitches can be worked in groups along an edge to create modular edges. For this edge, half the number of stitches required were cast on and the other half picked up along an edge. These stitches were then decreased to create a mitered square block (see page 73).

The triangle shape above is worked using the same technique as the square. Pick up stitches along the edge, using the tension to calculate the number of stitches across the length, and then for every following row, knit until two stitches remain and knit these two stitches together as for the second half of the square.

THREE-NEEDLE CAST-OFF

If the modules have live stitches along two or more edges, a useful cast-off and seam is the three-needle cast-off. It is quick but creates a ridge similar to that created by a seam. If one edge has live stitches and the other doesn't, consider picking up the same number of stitches along both edges.

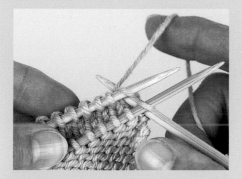

1 With right sides together, hold the two pieces to be joined in the left hand. Insert a third needle in the right hand through the stitch on the front, and then the corresponding stitch on the back needle in the left hand, and complete a knit stitch through both stitches. Repeat this with the next stitch on both needles.

2 With two stitch loops on the third needle, pass the first stitch, furthest from the tip, over the second to cast off. Insert the right needle through the next stitch on both left needles, complete a knit stitch, and repeat from the start of this step.

MOTIFS AND MEDALLIONS

Any stitch directory will have a range of motifs or medallions, but a few facts make understanding and selecting them easier.

Motifs and medallions are blocks that start with one stitch or a series of stitches and grow into a shape using increases. This shape is usually a regular-sided shape such as a square, octagon or triangle, which is easy to piece with other regular-sided shapes. Circular shapes are also popular but when pieced they do not create a solid fabric. The first stitch can be in the centre, a corner, or, in more unusual motifs, slightly to one side.

DESIGNING MOTIFS AND MEDALLIONS

If the motif or medallion is to be worked from the centre out, then it will start with a single stitch. To create a regular shape the increases will be positioned evenly and immediately above each other. The number of radiating columns of increases is equal to the number of sides the shape is to have. If the increase position is difficult to find then mark it using stitch markers or position double-pointed needles so that an increase falls at the end of a needle. The frequency of increase rows varies from knit to crochet and the stitch pattern and tension. For small square or round blocks about 15cm (6in) across, a rough guide to start experimental swatching is every round in crochet and every second row in knit sometimes with more, or more frequent, increases on shorter rows.

KNITTING A SQUARE FROM THE CENTRE OUT

Eight stitches were cast on and positioned on four needles, then an increase was worked at the beginning and end of each needle. In this case one round was knitted and the next purled, creating a garter stitch fabric in the round. The proportions of a garter stitch fabric dictate that increases are worked on every second round to create a flat square block.

△ **Modular motif**
This swatch uses the principles of a main motif that is created from the centre and then uses it to calculate how many stitches are required for the corner modules. It is attractive on both sides.

◁ **Modular chart**
This chart is a useful model for similar designs either within the same blanket or of your making.

▷ **Stocking stitch-based centre-out motif chart**
For a stocking stitch block, work increases at the beginning and end of each needle on every round for the first few shorter rounds, and then every second row (this will depend on the tension).

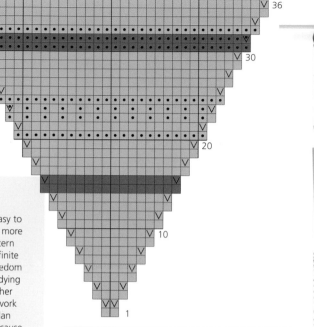

LACY MOTIFS

Lacy motifs or medallions are relatively easy to design because chains or yarnovers have more ease in them than solid stitches. The pattern set in this motif could continue for an infinite number of rounds, but to relieve the boredom other stitches can easily be added by studying the space the existing stitches take. In other words, use a basic motif such as this to work out the amount of space available and plan stitches. This basic motif is also useful because the twenty-four stitches on round two can be divided evenly to create an edge or side repeat for a four-sided, six-sided or eight-sided motif or medallion.

▽ **Changing shape**
To change this shape from a circle to a regular-sided shape, divide the number of stitches on the last round by the number of sides of the desired shape to find the frequency at which a double increase should be placed. The double increase is in fact one stitch for one side or edge and one stitch for another side or edge that meet at the point selected.

TIPS

One trick for working a stocking stitch square from the centre is to use smaller needles for the first few rounds and increase only every second round.

Knitting the first round on double-pointed needles is slightly easier if all the stitches are cast onto one needle, half the stitches are then transferred onto a second needle and the length is folded so the two end stitches are adjacent and near the needle tips. Check the number of stitches that will make a completed first round and divide this by the number of double-pointed needles you intend using, minus one. This gives the number of stitches on each needle. Using a third needle, start to work the first round into the first cast-on stitch until the number of stitches for each needle is on the third needle, then start to use the fourth needle. Continue in this manner until the first round is completed.

△ **Design possibilities of the centre-out motif**
This swatch has texture and stripes added with little effect on the increase-row frequency. Blocks are stored on bamboo skewers once completed and joined using a three-needle cast-off.

△ Log cabin from the centre

This motif or medallion features a colour change along each edge as the shape grows. In order for the colour to appear again without the breaking of the yarn there need to be five colours so the next same-colour edge appears one side around anticlockwise from the last.

△ Log cabin from a corner block

In this log cabin design, the additional strips are worked along the edge of previous strips. This is a useful way of using up odd scraps of yarn.

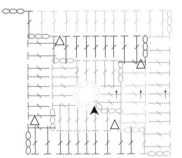

△ Log cabin from the centre chart

This motif does not appear as obviously as a motif with four panels divided by the need to create a corner. The increase and corner construction of this motif is a very useful technique to master as it does not produce a large hole or a rounded corner.

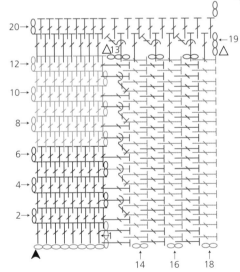

△ Log cabin from a corner block chart

The two block crochet swatches were based on this same chart. The number of rows worked for each strip dictates the construction. Each strip is six rows deep and the design progresses along alternate edges from a corner block.

△ Log cabin from a centre block

The principles of the log cabin have been adapted to a block of stitches to create a bolder design. The pattern set could continue to the size of a blanket – but remember, as the strips get the bigger so does the amount of yarn required. For a solid fabric the drape is exceptionally good in all directions. This is based on the same principle as the log cabin from a corner block but each strip is five rows deep so the design progresses anticlockwise.

▷ **Garter stitch and slip stitch knitting**
Garter stitch and slip-stitch stitch patterns are ideal for mitred squares, due to the fact that over two rows a stitch forms a square shape. The row of yarnovers is not sufficient to significantly distort the developing shape.

THE PRINCIPLE OF THE MITRED SQUARE

Each row increases the length of the outer selvedge edges by one along each edge and each increase increases the length of the worked edges by one along each edge. Think of a sheet of squared paper and how squares radiate from one corner.

MITRED BLOCKS

The principle of a mitred block is simple. It has either a double increase or a double decrease positioned in the centre of repeated increase or decrease rows, which allow a block to progress from a corner or from two sides to a corner. The principle is the same whether the block is knitted or crocheted, and in both cases a diagonal line of increases or decreases distinguishes these from motifs and medallions.

ADAPTING THE DESIGN

Any stitch pattern can be adapted to the mitred block ideal, but as with motifs and medallions, the frequency of the rows of increases or decreases will vary depending on the tension of the fabric. In knitting, one crucial design decision is the type of increase or decrease. In general, two stitches need to be decreased or increased every two rows. These can take the form of a double decrease: slip two stitches together, knit one, and pass the two slip stitches over; or two separate decreases slanting toward or away from the centre (see Knitted Lace Blocks, page 48). The increases can be made using yarnovers, make ones or increases.

▷ **Garter stitch and slip stitch knitting chart**
This swatch is worked from the outside in and uses double decreases over the centre stitch, creating a diagonal line of single stitches that appear to be at 45 degrees to the others. The centre of the decrease is slipped on the wrong side to create the chain on the garter stitch ground. To achieve this effect cast on double the number of stitches required for one edge of the block, plus one stitch.

ILLUSION KNITTING

Shadow knitting is where ridges of reverse stocking stitch create a shadow and when viewed from certain angles obscure part of the alternate stocking stitch stripes. The illusion of this kind of knitting is emphasized by using darker yarns and a strong contrast yarn. The reverse striping is also attractive as can be seen on the lower blocks of the shrug project, on page 128.

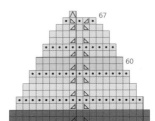

◁ **Shadow knitting chart**
This swatch is worked from the outside in and uses two decreases either side of a centre stitch creating a diagonal line of three stitches that appear to be at 45 degrees from the others. To achieve this effect cast on double the number of stitches required for one edge of the block, plus one stitch.

△ **Shadow knitting**
The knitted ridges in this swatch give an illusion of movement as it is viewed from different angles; this method is a simple way to make mitred squares more interesting.

KNITTING FROM THE OUTSIDE IN

For this method a tension has to be established for the yarn and needles used. Cast on double the number of stitches required for one edge of the block.

Knit half the stitches minus two stitches, knit two stitches together, place marker and knit two stitches together. Knit the following row. This swatch is a garter stitch swatch. If the block is to be worked in stocking stitch, work the decrease before the marker as a slip, slip, knit so the decreases both slant towards the centre.

TIP

Stripes and mitred blocks
A glance through a book of traditional patchwork fabric blocks will suggest numerous geometric possibilities for the mitred block. Both of these blocks have been made up of four smaller blocks, but the number of stripes and their depths differ to cleverly create two different designs.

◁ Crochet mitred square from the corner out
Double crochet is perfect for mitred squares because a single stitch is a square shape, and in order to make a square block the block has to increase in length along all its edges. All double crochet stitch patterns and stripes will work within this rule, but remember the stitch pattern will decrease by one stitch along each edge row, and working backwards and forwards means that each new edge won't necessarily be the start of the stitch pattern. Keep it simple.

▽ Crochet mitred square from the corner out chart
The corner is made up of one stitch for each edge and one stitch for the corner. For a lighter edge work one stitch for each edge and one or two chains for the corner stitch. Alternatively look at the corner turns of the log cabin motif on page 72; this will not produce a diagonal line of stitches but creates an interesting alternative look.

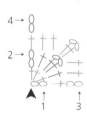

◁ Crochet mitred square from the outside in
The loop stitch in this swatch has been used to emphasize the diagonal and add texture. Two rows of loop stitch have also been worked when the outer edges were two-thirds of their final length.

▽ Crochet mitred square from the outside in chart
For this method, a tension must be established for the yarn and hook used. Cast on double the number of stitches required for one edge of the block. A larger hook was used to work the purple fluffy yarn to give more ease and restore the shape, which was becoming wayward. The fluffy yarn disguises the more open nature of the fabric.

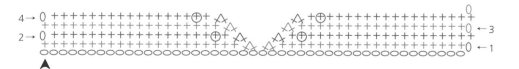

TIP

The crochet mitred square from the corner out (above) also had two rows of treble crochet filet – a useful design feature to keep in mind. These are not sufficient to distort the fabric but if the swatch is becoming distorted because the double crochet stitch height is not equal to its width then the chain and treble crochet stitches will help with their ease.

27 DESIGNING A BLANKET

There are several approaches to the design of a blanket; choose the one that works best for you.

Now that you have tried out some techniques and made some sample blocks, it's time to discuss the design of a blanket. Once you have worked a selection of blocks or pieces that you like, you can develop a design that is unique and original to you.

DESIGNING AN ALL-IN-ONE BLANKET

If you want to make an all-in-one blanket, take an objective look at the sample pieces you have made, and consider whether the yarn and the stitch pattern make the impact you want. Lay the piece(s) out flat (for example, on a bed) and look at the effect from the other side of the room as well as up close.

Consider adding some embroidery (see page 58), or extra panels or blocks around a central panel. Additional panels may be square, rectangular or perhaps triangular, as shown by the no-pattern block on page 69. Think too about how you will finish the edges, and consider the colour and texture of the finishing touches.

△ ▷ **Block orientation**
Even the simplest block design can be transformed by experimenting with its orientation.

MAKING DESIGN EASY

Squares of coloured paper or block photographs can be useful when designing a blanket.

Use the coloured paper squares to represent the dominant colour in selected blocks. (You can add extra detail with coloured pencils.) Alternatively, scan blocks from a printed source, or photograph your own sample, then use software to reduce the size of the image to about 2.5cm (1in) square and paste it several times onto a blank document. Print and cut out.

◁ **Flower baby blanket**
This blanket plays with texture in the yarns used, the drape of the fabric and the applied crochet flowers. The main section is worked in Old Shale (see page 46), and periodically lace rows were worked without the equal number of increases and decreases to create a flared shape. The shaping provides excellent drape and the extra fabric tucks neatly under a child's legs with no bulk around the arms. The flowers are secured firmly and provide endless entertainment.

DESIGNING A BLOCK BLANKET

As for the all-in-one blanket, lay out your sample pieces on a large flat area and review them objectively. Do any of them stand out more than others? Do any two look particularly good together? Is the drape evenly matched, or do some blocks require the support or drape of another? Remind yourself of the qualities that attracted you to each block and note any negative features.

Beginners may find it easier simply to take an existing design and change it; others may prefer either the logical or the intuitive approach.

THE LOGICAL APPROACH

This method starts with one, two or three blocks that are then repeated, rotated or reflected. Blocks may also be arranged to form a small group, which itself is then repeated, rotated or reflected.

THE INTUITIVE APPROACH

Start by taking a good look at the blocks and randomly selecting any combinations that catch your eye. Then alternate the blocks, rotate them and swap the blocks around. Each time you create an interesting group, make a note of it, either by making a small sketch, or using a digital camera. Perhaps your original arrangement will work the best, or maybe you will come up with an even more interesting combination of blocks.

The finished blanket design can either be an arrangement of interesting groups, or one or two groups repeated, rotated and reflected as described. The advantage of this way of designing is that it makes it easier to break away from symmetry, pattern and the predictable.

▷ **Using up odd balls of yarn**
The stripe design of this knitted throw was the perfect excuse to use up all the pink yarn left over from the numerous knitting projects for a baby girl. Some novelty yarn was incorporated to add interest. As shown here, a design plan can be as simple as choosing a palette of two contrasting colours.

▽ **Think outside the box**
Blankets do not have to be a regular shape and can be designed to enhance their environment or use.

DESIGN CHECKLIST

Size and shape
How big do you want your blanket to be? Will it be carried from place to place, or used for a certain purpose, in a particular situation? Is a square or rectangle the best shape? Would a round blanket be more interesting?

Practicality
The most important consideration is whether the blanket will be used by babies or small children. If so, avoid lacy stitches that can trap small fingers and toes, and consider using machine-washable yarn.

Colour
A selection of colours may be evenly spaced for a casual appearance, or graduated or grouped for a more formalized design. Groups of colours or tones can be used to suggest shapes. You may wish to complement the colour scheme of a room.

Drape
If the stitches on all the blocks run in the same direction, the drape in the direction of the stitches will behave differently from the drape across the stitches. You can avoid this effect by rotating blocks in a regular order, keeping the drape in balance.

Texture
The appearance and the feel of the blanket will be affected by the yarn and stitches you choose. Decide also how you want your blanket to feel — soft and cosy for a baby wrap, or firm and smooth for a toddler's play rug. Consider including contrasting textures, such as dress or upholstery fabric.

28 FINISHING

Racing to the finish is almost inevitable, but you should take as much care at this stage as at any other; after all, you will have invested a lot of time and effort in your project.

The golden rule, never to be broken, is: do not stay up late to finish a project or be tempted to "just" sew a few seams together to see how they will look. Mistakes will happen!

BLOCKING

Just as with working a tension swatch, it can be tempting to skip the blocking stage. It sounds laborious because it involves the pinning of the pieces shape-perfect and then setting that shape. But imagine what has happened to that beautiful ball of yarn: you have worked it in a good mood and in a bad mood, it has been scrunched into bags, carted around, pulled, tugged and admired then stashed away until this final stage. It needs to be revived. Just treat the blocking process as an excuse to admire the work further.

Start with a blocking surface. For blocks this can be simply an ironing board; but only if it can be devoted to blocking for a while. Alternatives include a single mattress – again only if not in constant use – a heavy rug with a protective towel pinned out or a homemade or bought blocking board. Making a blocking board is not difficult. It is just a piece of hardboard, with one side covered with two or three layers of quilter's batting and a piece of checked fabric. The fabric provides a grid along which the corners of a block or worked pieces can be aligned. The important thing to remember is that whatever you use should be fairly heat-tolerant.

SEAMING

Blocking all the pieces will make seaming easier. Blankets, after all, are tricky to seam because both sides may be on show and so it is important that the seam is even and neat. Fortunately there are some tricks to help.

First, choose the right seam stitch. There are two basic types: the no-nonsense, minimal visual impact seam (see opposite) and the feature seam, including crocheted seams, seams in a contrasting yarn and lacy inserts (see pages 80 to 85).

SEAMING METHOD

The drape of the completed blanket can be affected by the order and method in which blocks are seamed. As with everything else in its construction, similar elements of the blanket should be treated the same. First, pin the adjacent edges of two blocks together starting with the corners and then easing the fabric between. Using safety pins at this stage will provide a more secure and accurate hold as well as allowing the edges to be positioned edge to edge. Then, pin several blocks together to create a larger block and seam across all the blocks in one direction across the blanket widthwise. Next, seam across all the blocks in the other direction from head to foot. Continue to work in similar sized blocks, seaming in one direction first and then the other, across the whole blanket. Piece these larger blocks in the same way. Alternatively, piece the blanket in vertical strips, then join the strips together, which produces a particularly good drape from head to foot. These methods of seaming will also improve the appearance on the reverse.

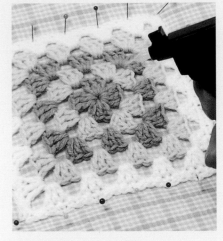

BLOCKING A SQUARE

Start by referring to the pattern or tension swatch to discover the dimensions of the square and check the ball band for any care instructions with reference to blocking or pressing.

1 Using rustproof pins, pin out the square to the correct size right side up.
2a For natural fibres, use steam from an iron to set the shape. Hold the iron just above the surface, then working in sections and with a constant flow of steam, hover across the surface of the block.
2b For synthetic or mixed fibres, use a spray bottle to dampen the block with cold water.
3 Allow the block to dry thoroughly before removing the pins.

BLOCKING ALL-IN-ONE PIECE BLANKETS

Size is no excuse to skip the blocking step. The best option is to use a very large surface such as a bed mattress or a rug. (Ensure that whatever surface you use is heat resistant.) If this really isn't possible then employ the ironing board, a warm iron and a damp cloth. Work in sections on the wrong side, gently pressing the blanket and avoiding any textured areas.

SEAMING CAST-OFF EDGE TO CAST-ON EDGE

1 Thread a tapestry needle with matching yarn and working from the back of the work to the front and from right to left, bring the needle up through the centre of the first stitch on the last row of the bound-off edge.

2 From the front and from right to left pass the needle under the two loops of the first stitch of the cast-on edge.

3 From the front and from right to left, insert the needle back down through the centre of the last stitch sewn on the bound-off edge and up through the centre of the next stitch. Then pass the needle under the two loops of the next stitch of the cast-on edge. Repeat to the end of the row.

SEAMING SELVEDGE TO SELVEDGE

1 Thread a tapestry needle with matching yarn and start either by working a figure of eight between the first two stitches or leaving a tail to be woven into the completed seam. From the front and from bottom to top pass the needle under two horizontal bars towards the inside of the first stitch.

2 From the front and from bottom to top pass the needle under two horizontal bars towards the inside of the first stitch on the opposite edge.

TIP

Some people prefer to block right-side up, and some prefer to block right-side down. With the right side up it is possible to smooth the stitches and pull them slightly to get an even fabric before it dries. If you take care, it is also easier not to flatten the texture with this method.

Leave the weaving in of ends until all the seams have been sewn then, wherever possible, weave the ends into the base of the seam flaps.

MATTRESS STITCH

From the right-side, a mattress-stitch seam is almost invisible, but on the wrong side it creates two short flaps. Work it with the right-side facing.

WOVEN SEAM CROCHET

This seam is more limited than mattress stitch in that it can only be worked with either foundation chain edges or the top chain formed by the last row of stitches; but it does work well with medallions. From the right side this seam is almost invisible, but on the wrong side it creates two discreet flaps. Work it with the wrong side facing.

Thread a tapestry needle with matching yarn and with the foundation chain edge to the right and the last row of stitches on the left, pass the needle under the two stitch loops of the foundation chain on the right side. Then pass the needle under the corresponding two top chain loops of the last row of stitches on the other edge. Repeat to the end of the line of stitches.

29 DECORATIVE SEAMS

The seams are going to show on at least one side of the fabric, so you could choose to include them in the design and make a feature of them.

Seams offer a useful visual and engineering framework to a blanket. Just as the staves of a chair may be turned, or the structural elements of a building may be carved and decorated, so the seams of a blanket can be worked and displayed with pride.

CROCHETED SEAMS

Crocheted seams are among the quickest and easiest ways of joining the pieces of a blanket. They create a small ridge on the side that is facing as you work – either the right side or the wrong side – but if worked in a contrasting yarn they can easily be made into a feature. Crocheted seams work equally well along side edges as along start and finish edges, and along crochet edges as well as knit edges. Just make sure to keep the distance visually equal between each stitch, and once a pattern of stitch placement is established make a note of it and continue in the same manner over the whole blanket.

△ **Double crochet seam**
Working through the back loops only creates a less dense and more flexible seam.

△ **Slip stitch seam**
A slip stitch seam is basically surface crochet used to join two pieces together. A slip stitch crochet seam doesn't stand proud of the two joined edges as a double crochet or crab stitch seam would. When a seam is reached that crosses the seam being worked remove the hook from the loop, insert the hook through the fabric from the direction of the seam to the loop. Draw the loop through and continue along the seam.

TIP

Working a slip stitch seam through the back loops only and in the same direction on both loops produces a seam with no ridge and a running stitch line on the right side of the work. It could be described as a surface crochet seam.

CRAB STITCH SEAM

Crab stitch is sometimes also known as reverse double crochet.

1 Place the two blocks right sides together so that the seam will appear on the wrong side. Working from left to right insert the hook under the top stitch loops of the corresponding stitches on each piece from front to back and wrap the yarn over the hook.

2 Draw the yarn through from back to front.

3 Wrap the yarn over the hook and draw it through the two loops on the hook to complete the stitch.

△ Not-so-discreet mattress stitch

Mattress stitch produces two flaps on the wrong side. These can be displayed on the right side by working mattress stitch with the wrong side facing. To make a feature of this seam work a selvedge of a knit stitch at the beginning or end of each row or oversew the side edges of the knitted piece.

△ Thrice-worked seam

The two back loops have been treble crocheted to secure the edges and the front loops have been worked in single crochet to create a fan effect. This seam is very bulky.

△ Partial seaming

These blocks have only been partially joined by a surface crochet spiral. This creates a blanket with a lighter drape than if all the edges had been fully seamed.

△ Beaded seam

The occasional beaded seam can be attractive, but the cumulative weight of all the seams being beaded would be high. This seam is a slip stitch seam through the back loops only.

▽ Contrasting colour

The slip stitch seam has been worked in a contrasting colour echoing a design element in the block.

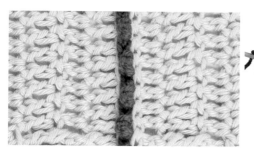

△ Picot edging

There is no reason why an edging cannot be applied to a seam. It does increase the bulk and the drape across the seam will not be as good, but it is another decorative option.

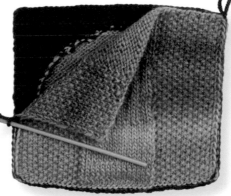

△ Secret pockets

Two knitted blocks have been joined through back loops to hide the untidy stranding on one block. This can then be seamed to neighbouring blanket blocks through the front loops. If only three sides are joined a useful pocket may be formed.

30 LACY SEAMS

Decorative, practical, and lightweight, lacy seams are
a prettier, more delicate option than ordinary seams.

"Lacy seams" are either for joining lace or
are seams where a group of stitches form a
lightweight strip or narrow section of inserted
fabric between two blocks.

When and where are always the questions
with lacy seams. On heavy, dense blankets
they improve the drape, on lacy blankets they
maintain the lightness and joining picots on
medallions creates an almost imperceptible join.
However, on a heavyweight blanket the weight
of the blocks may distort and stretch these
delicate seams, and their tendency to catch

makes them unsuitable for blankets in constant
use or those that require frequent laundering.

The inserted strips of fabric are more
commonly crocheted. However, it is also
possible to join two blocks using knitted lace
if at the end of each row of the insert a stitch
is picked up along the edge of the block to be
joined. This is then knitted together at the
beginning of the next row with the first stitch
on the lace insert. Of course, a knitted strip
can be worked and then seamed between
two blocks as well as any crocheted strip.

△ **Double crochet lace seam**
This seam does not look like a lace seam because
the fabric between the two blocks appears quite
dense, but because alternate stitches are worked
on alternate blocks, the inserted stitching is flexible
and light. This is a strong lace insert.

JOINING LACE MOTIFS USING PICOTS

Crochet medallions can be sewn together along the entire length of an edge, but some – in particular
those with an irregular edge – are joined through picot loops on their last round. This is a very quick
and efficient method of joining and it does not make them any less portable; it simply means that
medallion blocks can be carried out and about until their penultimate round, and then are joined
to their neighbour later when it is convenient.

△ **Double crochet lace seam chart**
Start with the right sides facing outwards and the
edges held together facing upwards. Working right
to left, join the seam yarn under both top loops of
the first stitch of the front medallion and work three
chains. Work the next stitch under the top loops of
the first stitch on the back medallion and then work
the following stitch into the position indicated on
the front medallion. Continue working alternate
stitches in alternate medallions in this manner
until the two medallions are joined.

1 Complete the first medallion. Work the second
medallion to the point in the last round at which it would
meet the first medallion in the completed blanket. Place
the two medallions together wrong sides facing with the
second medallion in front. Work half the picot chain, slip
stitch or treble crochet around the picot of the first motif,
and complete the picot chain of the second motif.

2 Complete the second motif, repeating the join at any
other points where the second medallion meets the
first. Work the remaining medallions in the same way,
joining to any adjacent completed medallions in the
last round of the medallion.

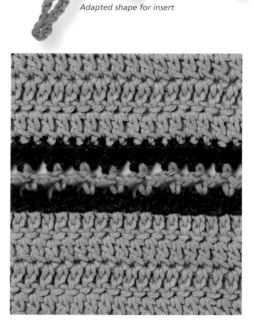

Adapted shape for insert

△ Joining lace motifs using a second shape or insert

Some medallion shapes do not tessellate to form an even fabric. In these cases a design often includes a pattern for a smaller design, which fits into the space. This second shape can be worked in a matching or contrasting colour or even a contrasting yarn, blending or contrasting with the neighbouring shapes.

△ Inserted shape chart

Any small design can be adapted to become an insert by creating and extending or shortening chains with a picot at its apex. These can then be joined to their neighbouring medallions.

△ Filet lace worked along the edge

This filet lace design was worked the length of the edge and slip stitched in place between the two blocks.

◁ Filet chart along the edge

The length of the edges to be joined has to be accurately determined before working a foundation chain.

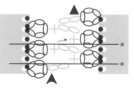

△ Filet lace worked across the seam

This filet lace design was worked across the width of the gap between the two blocks and then joined to each block by a series of double crochet stitches, with the right sides facing outwards.

◁ Filet chart along the edge

Thread the beads onto the yarn before working the pattern. The length of the insert is easily adjusted.

△ Picot lace seam

In this lace seam, a picot edging is worked on both edges and these are joined with a contrasting yarn.

△ Picot lace seam chart

Edgings can be adapted to create a seam between two blocks. Colours can either match or contrast with those of the blocks.

TIP

Supporting the two edges
with a darning mushroom
can make seaming easier.
Before searching the stores
for a darning mushroom,
you may want to try the
technique using a smooth,
fist-sized ball; a leather
juggling ball works well.

TR SEAM

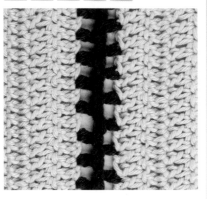

As the stitches are worked on both
edges, every second stitch or stitch width,
this is a strong seam. Fairly neutral in
appearance, work it along any two edges
in a contrasting or matching yarn.
Try placing a bead halfway through a
treble crochet stitch or using variegated
yarns to change the look.

With right sides facing, join in yarn on the
bottom corner of the left-hand edge.
Foundation chain: ch 3.
Cont to work from the chart, alternating
sts between the right and left side as
directed, and working from the bottom to
the top of the seam.
Fasten off.

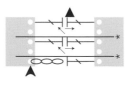

CHAIN ZIGZAG

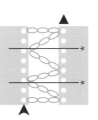

Care should be taken with this seam
because it is attached only every third
stitch to each edge and the chain is
vulnerable to snagging. If the seam is
not held fairly taut, either by its own
weight or smoothed over a bed, it can
look messy. The chain count and
spacing are easily adjusted to suit
individual requirements.

With right sides facing, join in yarn on the
bottom corner of the left-hand edge.
Foundation chain: ch 3.
Cont to work from the chart, alternating
sts between the right and left side as
directed and working from the bottom to
the top of the seam.
Fasten off.

TR ZIGZAG

This edging demonstrates how two
edgings can be combined. This is a very
light and lacy edge that can either be
used to lighten a blanket with an
otherwise heavy drape or harmonize in a
lacy blanket that would be ruined if heavy
seams were used.

With right sides facing, join in yarn on the
bottom corner of the left-hand edge.
Foundation chain: ch 3.
Cont to work from the chart, alternating
sts between the right and left side as
directed and working from the bottom to
the top of the seam.
Fasten off.

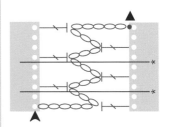

BOBBLY SEAM

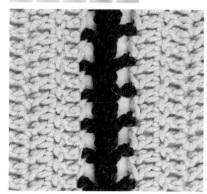

This textured edging provides the light drape of a lacy seam because of the infrequency with which it attaches to either edge. The texture is particularly pleasing when it provides a contrast with smooth fabrics.

With wrong sides facing, join in yarn on the top corner of the right-hand edge.
Foundation chain: ch 3.
Cont to work from the chart, alternating sts between the right and left side as directed and working from the bottom to the top of the seam.
Fasten off.

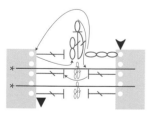

LACE SEAM

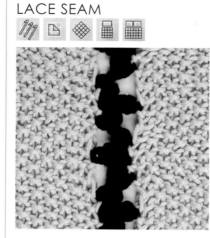

The idea for this seam came from an edging stitch pattern found in *The Crochet Stitch Bible* by Betty Barnden. The seam was started at the highest part of the pattern to set the width of the seam and alternate groups of stitches were worked along each edge. To make the seam more open, increase the distance between the slip stitches.

With right sides facing, join in yarn on the bottom corner of the left-hand edge.
Foundation chain: ch 3.
Cont to work from the chart, alternating sts between the right and left side as directed and working from the bottom to the top of the seam.
Fasten off.

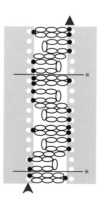

BEADED SEAM

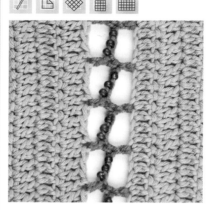

Beaded seams work well towards the outside of a blanket because they add some weight, but too many can quickly make a blanket uncomfortably heavy. Beads can be used to adorn any stitch pattern, but remember that if a bead is slipped to the base of the hook between chain stitches it will appear on the reverse of the side you are working on.

Thread the beads onto the yarn.
With wrong sides facing, join in yarn on the bottom corner of the left-hand edge.
Foundation chain: ch 3.
Cont to work from the chart, alternating sts between the right and left side as directed and working from the bottom to the top of the seam.
Fasten off.

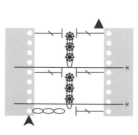
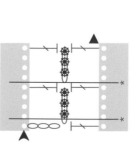

The ease in a lacy seam makes it ideal for joining irregular edges, for example between a lacy block and a more solid one, to create a smooth finish.

A lacy seam can also be used to continue the lightness of two adjacent lacy blocks.

KEY

Make cluster, ch 2, 2trtog, in the sp below the base of the ch-2 and between the last 2 tr sts worked.

Place the bead, slide the bead along the yarn to the base of the hook and work the next stitch as directed by the pattern.

EDGINGS AND TRIMMINGS

There are stitch directories full of decorative edgings, but here are a few techniques and ideas that will help with the making and selection.

Edgings or trimmings are a useful way of unifying a design and adding strength to the vulnerable edge of a finished blanket. Their weight and shape can also improve the drape, with a wavy or pointed edging having concentrations of greater weight.

There are two types of edgings: those that are worked from the edge of a fabric (the number of rows worked will determine the depth) and those that are worked in a narrow strip and applied to the edge of fabric (the number of stitches worked will determine the depth).

TIP

When working an edging separately from the fabric to be edged, do not fasten off the stitches until the edge has been attached to the blanket edge, so the length can still be adjusted if necessary.

KNITTING FROM AN EDGE

The main concern with this kind of edging is holding the stitches. If the blanket you are making is large, you will need several circular needles, and point protectors as stoppers. The weight can be tiring on the arms and wrists. Luckily, the neat edging shown on this page, whose depth can be easily adjusted as you work, is well worth the effort. Start by piecing a block blanket or casting off an all-in-one blanket. The seam created is a useful strengthening framework. Once all the edges are cast off and pieced, it is just a matter of picking up stitches along each edge and working the edging pattern of your choice.

APPLYING TO AN EDGE

The beauty of the self-contained edge, attached as a separate entity, is that it is a narrow strip, which means it is light and easy to transport, but the only adjustment that can be made as it is being worked is its length and the corner details. These strip edging patterns tend to be more elaborate, but you should look for patterns with a fairly short row repeat so that it need only be stretched slightly to end at a corner. A short row repeat may sound boring, but remember that only a small number of stitches is worked, so progress will be fast. In most cases, strip edgings then need to be attached to the blanket. This can be done decoratively (see page 80) or with mattress stitch (see page 79). In either case, consider using a selvedge stitch on the edge to be attached to the blanket.

▽ **Simple beaded edging**
The beads in this simple strip edging add some weight as well as sparkle.

◁ **Beaded edging chart**
This edging is worked from the edge of a crochet fabric by picking up stitches and working simple garter stitch stripes. A single row of beads is added by sliding them along the yarn one at a time as directed and placing them at the base of the needle between the stitches as indicated.

▽ **Simple knitted pintuck edge**
This type of edging is robust and will provide a strong edge to a blanket. The row of yarnovers and decreases adds flexibility to the edging.

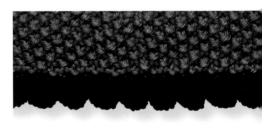

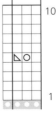

◁ **Pintuck chart**
This edging is worked from the edge of a knitted fabric by picking up stitches and working from the chart. Row 11 is worked by picking up, with the left-hand needle, the loop below the next stitch on the reverse of the fabric created by the stitch picked up ten rows before. This is then knitted together with the next stitch on the needle. This is repeated along the row.

PICKING UP STITCHES TO KNIT

First work a gauge swatch of the edging in the yarn to be used. Count the number of stitches over the distance of 15cm (6in) and this will become the number of stitches to be picked up along the same distance of the knitted or crocheted fabric. Then pick up and work the edging along a gauge swatch of the fabric to be edged. This is useful for two reasons: first, it gives a better impression of how the edging will look, and second it allows you to experiment with the stitch placement along the edge to achieve the desired count. For instance, pick up a stitch in the next two stitches or rows and then miss a stitch or row. Establishing this kind of rhythm will produce a neater finish, but remember to keep a note of it.

◁ ▽ **Simple reversible knitted cable pattern**
This edging is worked separately from the blanket, folded in half and seamed to form a tube using mattress stitch, and then attached to crochet fabric using whip stitch.

△ **Along a cast-on or cast-off edge**
Working from right to left, insert the tip of the right-hand needle through the centre of the first stitch on the edge of the fabric, wrap the yarn around the needle as if to knit, and pull the loop through the fabric so it sits on the needle. Repeat to the end of the row.

△ **Along row edge**
Working from right to left, insert the tip of the right-hand needle between the first two stitches on the edge of the fabric, wrap the yarn around the needle as if to knit, and pull the loop through the fabric so it sits on the needle. Repeat to the end of the row.

△ **Reversible edging chart**
The ideas for a reversible stitch pattern can also be applied to the edgings. The rib stitch pattern is made up of one knit stitch followed by one purl stitch over 14 stitches. Then, keeping the pattern correct, a cable-eight-back is worked every fifth row.

PICKING UP KNIT STITCHES TO JOIN AN EDGING

It is possible to join an edging that needs to be applied to a blanket edge as you work the edging. The main problem is turning the work, which includes both the edging and the blanket, but there are plenty of sources of information on how to knit backwards from the right-hand needle onto the left-hand needle.

Work the edgings as directed, but at the end of each row the edging will meet the blanket. Pick up one stitch. Turn the work and on the next row work the picked-up stitch loop and the first edging stitch together.

The beads are added on the side not attached to the blanket by threading them onto the yarn before the edging is started and, at the start of each row on that edge, by sliding a bead to the base of the last stitch and working the first stitch of the row through the back of the stitch.

CROCHET EDGINGS

Even steadfast knitters acknowledge that a crochet edging is one of the prettiest ways to finish a blanket.

Crochet edgings are useful because crochet is so adaptable. It is easy to adjust distances and chain lengths without visibly distorting the pattern. The addition of chains or extra stitches allows an edging to remain flexible, and the finished result of the same basic stitch pattern concept can be as light as a feather, providing a gentle drape, or solid and immovable, providing a strong scaffold.

Unlike in knitting, where each stitch must be worked in a particular way on each row, in crochet a stitch pattern can be adapted to fit the circumstances. If it doesn't work, it is easy to return to the point at which it was going well. Crochet stitch patterns are more of a notion of how stitches should link to each other and the spacing between is just waiting to be adapted.

CROCHET FROM AN EDGE

Working from an edge is much easier in crochet than in knitting because there is only one loop to worry about. However, it is still not the most portable solution. The only consolation is that crochet generally works an area faster than knitting.

CROCHET ACROSS AN EDGE

Unlike knitting, these edges are rarely worked separately and attached later. There is no reason to when a simple slip stitch will secure it to the blanket at the end of every alternate row.

△ **Simple crochet pintuck edge**
Pintucks provide stability and a strong edge. They can be made more flexible but less durable by increasing the spacing between the stitches. They can be made to act like a scaffold by working them more tightly. This edge has been worked in contrasting colours, which will be glimpsed if the blanket is displayed casually.

◁ **Crisp pintuck edge chart**
The neatest form of pintuck for an edge requires that the first pintuck row of stitches is worked through the front loop only, the second through the back loop, and the third row of stitches is either a slip stitch or a double crochet stitch worked through both loops of the last row and the back loop of the first pintuck row.

CROCHETING FROM LIVE KNIT STITCHES

This is a very useful technique when you want a crochet edging but no seam created by binding off the stitches and then crocheting into the fabric. This particularly complements a knitted blanket with a light drape and few other seams, but for a light strengthening along the edge, work the first row or round in double crochet.

With the right side facing and working right to left, work any yarn over hook wraps required for the crochet stitch to be worked on the first row or round and insert the hook into the knit stitch loop from front to back. Complete the crochet stitch.

△ **Beaded pintuck**
Beads have been added to this stout pintuck edge. The beads provide a focus, as well as adding weight and perhaps sound as the edge hits a hard surface.

◁ **Beaded pintuck chart**
The two rows of stitches of different stitch heights mean that the edge of the pintuck is two-thirds up the length of the treble crochet stitch.

TIP

Echo a stitch pattern in the blanket along the edge but use a larger hook to create a sympathetic lacy edging.

△ Beaded loops

A trellis-like stitch is one of the simplest lace edgings that can be added to a blanket. This edging without the beads provides a hint of decoration and gives the edges a uniform appearance; the beads add the weight to improve the drape and the decorative interest. Too many beads may distort the shape of the edge and make the blanket less comfortable.

△ Beaded loops chart

This is an excellent method of attaching beads because the chains on which they hang allow the beads some freedom of movement. Thread the beads onto the yarn and, when a bead is indicated, remove the hook from the loop, insert the hook through the next bead from the side furthest from the loop, insert the hook through the loop and draw the loop through the bead. For larger beads, increase the number of chains; for smaller beads, reduce the number of chains.

△ Thrice-worked edge

This edge works best on an edge with a chain, either from the foundation chain or the last row or round of crochet or the cast-off or chain selvedge of knitted fabric. The first row of stitches (yellow) is worked through the front loop of the edge, and the second run of stitches (blue) is worked through the back loop of the same edge. The two innermost loops are then worked (red). The double crochet stitch in this example gives a tight finish, but the same process with a treble crochet stitch gives a more flexible edge.

△ Loop edging to ruffle

This edging is created by working short lengths of front post stitches (see Flower on page 116), which are secured with treble crochet stitches to the edge. Towards the left, the loops are spaced by three treble crochet stitches between each loop; on the right, a loop is started in one stitch position and finished in the next. The following loop starts in the next stitch position. The removal of a few stitches from a stitch pattern repeat changes a loop edging into a ruffle.

TIP

Have a cable needle or a smaller hook to hand to help prise a position through the yarn strands of the stitch posts along a crochet edge. Alternatively, make a chain and work the space on a subsequent row. Whichever method you use, be consistent.

△ Ruffled up the wrong way

This loop stitch pattern is similar to the loop one above, but the yarn is a heavy weight for the pattern, the front post lengths are very short and each stitch position has been worked. Rather than a ruffle, a rope-like edging has been created that will wear well, but it will distort the edge if it is worked over a long length.

CHART REMINDER

To read a chart, start at the bottom right and read odd-numbered rows (right side rows) from right to left and even-numbered rows (wrong side rows) from left to right (see pages 26–27). To each repeat total, add stitches to the foundation chain for the turning chain. This turning chain is also the first stitch.

KEY

⬇   Pick up a stitch through an edge loop.

③   Slide the number of beads stated along the yarn, to the base of the right-hand needle between the two stitches indicated.

FAIR ISLE PINTUCK

The beauty of this technique is that it conceals the fabric edge. It is possible to work the corners by increasing by one stitch either side of a corner stitch until row 8 and then working one decrease either side of the corner stitch until the cast-off. However, it is simpler to work two opposite edges separately and then repeat the edging along the remaining edges and the sides of the first two runs of edging.

Using yarn A, join in yarn and pick up and knit sts evenly along the fabric edge.
Cont to work from the chart.
Cast off: [pick up with the left-hand needle, the loop on the reverse of the fabric created by the picked-up st 16 rows below the next stitch on the needle, k tog with then next st on the needle] twice, pass the second st on the right-hand needle over the first. *Pick up with the left-hand needle, the next loop on the reverse of the fabric, k tog with then next st on the needle, pass the second st on the right-hand needle over the first, rep from * to the end of the row.

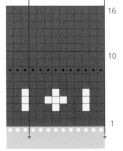

Colours: dark pink (A) and cream (B)
Repeat: 10 sts plus 3 sts

BEADING FLAIR

The beads add sparkle to a blanket edge. It is easy to adapt the spacing and the bead combinations to create a different look. The beads will add weight, but using plastic or wooden beads can lessen this. Launder this edging carefully.

Thread beads onto the yarn.
Join in yarn and pick up sts evenly along the fabric edge.
Cont to work from the chart.
*Cast off until the first group of beads, [yo pass the last l p on the right-hand needle over] 3 times, rep from * to the end of the row.

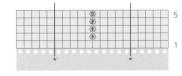

Repeat: 12 sts

BUNTING

This edging and its variations are very popular. It is easy to adapt and often works when nothing else will. Just adapt the depth of it – the number of stitches the row is allowed to increase to before the row stitch total is decreased every second row. Placing a bead at the beginning of each right side row or the beginning of the row that marks the apex of the triangle are effective variations.

Using the thumb method, cast on 3 sts and pick up 1 st in the fabric to be edged. This completes row 1 (RS).
Cont to work from the chart, starting with row 2 and reading from the left.
Rep the charted rows until the desired length is reached.
Cast off.
Using a double strand of yarn B, work first one French knot on one side and then work a second French knot on the reverse side, into the centre of alternate triangles.
Rep using yarn C.

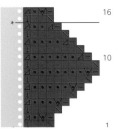

Colours: red (A), yellow (B) and blue (C)
Repeat: 14 rows plus 2 rows

ZIGZAG WAVE

As with all edgings, the appearance of this one can change dramatically by adjusting the spacing on the initial row of chain stitches and slip stitches into the fabric. Closer together, a denser ruffle-type edging is produced. If the space between each slip stitch is increased, the zigzag nature of the edging becomes more apparent. This edging also lends itself to being worked twice along an edge with the initial slip stitches of the second edging being worked in between the slip stitches of the first edging. The zigzag can be deepened or shortened by altering the length of the initial chain. Beads along the second row, or at the points only, would work well.

Join in yarn with a sl st and work ch and sl sts evenly along the fabric edge. Cont to work from the chart. Fasten off.

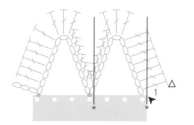

Repeat: 15 sts

BROOMSTICK EDGING

This edging provides a soft but firm edging and is one found on many baby blankets from 30 or 40 years ago. It is the perfect base for further embellishment, either with beads as the loops are worked, or surface embroidery and drawn thread work once the edging has been completed. The edging shown was worked around a stiff tape measure that reached along the edge of the fabric.

Join in yarn with a sl st and double crochet evenly along the fabric edge. Cont to work from the chart. Fasten off.

Repeat: 1 st

FAUX FRINGE

This edging demonstrates how, if a pattern is broken for a period along an edge, it becomes less of a texture, especially with a fringe edging such as this one. This edging pattern has regular breaks, but the spacing distances could be varied and a second pattern introduced in between.

Join in yarn with a sl st and double crochet evenly along the fabric edge.
Rows 1–2: ch 2 (counts as 1 dc), 1 dc into each st to the end of the row, work the last dc into the 1st ch of the beg ch before turning.
Row 3: *[work the chart rep] 4 times and finish the rep with the last sts indicated, sc into each of the next 3 sts, rep from * to the end of the row.
Fasten off.

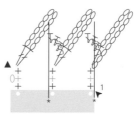

Repeat: 10 sts plus 7 sts

WAVY BROOMSTICK EDGING

The broomstick edging described left has been worked into every stitch on a knit fabric. This stitch spacing is closer than usual for a flat crochet edging worked along a knitted fabric edge even if, as in this case, the yarn weights are equal. This has created a wave effect.

KEY

Working from left to right, insert the hook into the fl of the next st, yo, draw the yarn through, and place the l p onto the needle or strip of card.

EDGING CORNERS

Corners are the turning-point of a successful edging.

A corner can be simply an extension of an edging or it can be a focal point, a statement in itself. You can create a corner by edging each side of a blanket and leaving the sides of the edgings exposed at the corners to form V-shaped gaps. If the blanket is for a bed this allows the edging to hang straight down at the corners. (The edging does need to be fairly deep or with some weight for this to be effective.) The V-shaped gap may be filled with a tassel or a block shape or two. For example, adding a square block would create a corner frill.

MATCHING CORNERS TO EDGINGS

If the corners are to reflect the edging worked along the fabric, the simplest corner treatment is to edge two opposite sides, then work the remaining edgings along the edge of the worked fabric, and the sides of the edgings already applied. It works, but the corners tend not to drape well and the sides of the last edgings are exposed.

The stitch marker marks the beginning of the round. It's easier to work a mitred edge from an edge rather than a corner.

▷ **Knitted edging corner**
Edgings can be used on a block and an edging that is worked all the way around changes a block which is slightly too small or with a strong drape in one direction into a block that can have a more flexible drape and live stitches all the way around for attaching to its neighbour with the three-needle cast-off technique (see page 69). This edging uses a garter stitch stripe for added visual movement; colours are obscured and revealed as the block moves.

If you are planning to work a three-needle cast-off, bamboo skewers are a useful way of holding the live stitches of a block until they can be joined to its neighbour.

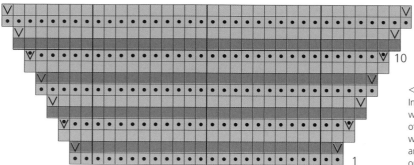

◁ **Knitted edging corner chart**
In edgings worked from an edge, the simplest way to work a corner is first to pick up a stitch in the corner of the block or blanket, and mark it as a corner stitch with a stitch marker. Then, on subsequent rows, work an increase either side of the corner stitch. This chart only shows one edge and is repeated four times.

OTHER CORNER SOLUTIONS

Other methods allow the continuous working of an edge and working a corner into the edging pattern. For an edging that is worked from an edge, block designs worked from the centre or corner out are a good source of inspiration, with extra stitches and spaces at the corners. For edgings that are attached to an edge, extra rows need to be added at the corner.

TURNING A FLAT CORNER EDGING INTO A FRILL

Extra full rows attached to the same stitch will turn flat edging into a frill. This method turns a ruffle or frill into something that resembles a tutu, so consider a less frilly design at the corners, or simply allow the frill to turn the corners and become flatter. Extra weight at the corners is useful to help them hang straight, but short rows are a better solution for attached edgings.

WORKING A CROCHET EDGING CORNER

EXTRA STITCHES

A common way to work a corner in crochet is to work extra stitches into the corner space. In this example, the last stitch along one edge, three extra corner stitches, and the first stitch of the following fabric edge are worked into the same place. The number of stitches is determined by the height of the stitch. A double crochet stitch usually only needs one extra stitch, and a double treble often needs six or seven. On subsequent rounds, the sequence of edge and extra corner stitches is repeated on the new corner apex, which is the centre extra stitch or space on the previous round.

EXTRA CHAIN STITCHES

Another method of working a corner is to work extra chain stitches or a space into the corner space. In this example, the last stitch along one edge, three extra corner chain stitches, and the first stitch of the following fabric edge are worked into the same place. The length of the chain is determined by the height of the stitch and is usually equivalent to what you would allow for a turning chain at the beginning of a row. On subsequent rounds the new corner apex is the corner space on the previous round, and the sequence of edge and chain stitches is worked into the space.

MITRED CORNERS

Corners are slightly more difficult to make in edgings that are worked in a long strip and have to be attached at the end of the row or with a sewn seam. The neatest way to turn a corner is to work a series of short rows or rows that are only partially worked before the work is turned, and the stitches just worked are worked again.

Work until you reach the corner, then, starting from the edge that will be on the outside and not joined to the fabric, work the row until two stitches remain on the left-hand needle. Wrap the next stitch, turn the work and work back along the row to the end. On the next row and every subsequent alternate row work one stitch less than the last alternate row until only one stitch is worked. On every subsequent alternate row work one more stitch than the last alternate row, lifting the wrapped loop around the slipped stitch onto the left-hand needle. Working it together with the previously slipped stitch, knit two together, turn the work, and work the return row. Repeat until all the stitches are worked and the original row length is restored.

△ **Short-row mitre with wrapped stitches**
On stocking stitch-based edgings more than about 12 stitches deep, some experimentation will be required to achieve a flat corner, as a stocking stitch is not square and fewer short rows than there are stitches will be required. Knitting the wrapped loop and the slipped stitch together as a knit two together on a corner turning to the left creates a slight texture along the mitre. For a smoother fabric, work a left-slanting decrease such as slip-slip-knit on the wrap and slip stitch.

△ **Short-row mitre with yarnovers**
Yarnovers create a flexible mitre, which is more tolerant of stitch patterns as the yarnover length adjusts slightly to create a flat fabric. The principles are the same as for a wrapped stitch short row: work a row of reduced length and, at the beginning of the return row, work a yarnover.

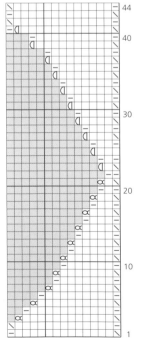

◁ **Short-row mitre with wrapped stitches chart**
Work to the point at which the corner has been reached and work the first short row. On the next row work about four-fifths of the row and count fewer stitches before wrapping the next stitch and turning the work. Repeat this on the next short row. On every subsequent short row work one stitch less than the last alternate row until only one stitch is worked. Increase the length of the short rows by working to the first wrapped stitch on the row, lifting the wrap, and working it together with the slip stitch, before turning the work and working the return row. Continue until all the wrapped stitches have been worked.

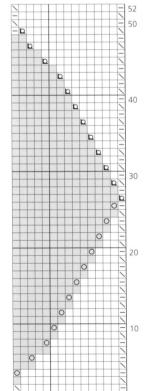

◁ **Short-row mitre with yarnovers chart**
As the row lengths reduce, work the yarnover at the beginning of the row as short as possible by wrapping it clockwise round the right-hand needle before proceeding along the return row. To achieve a smoother mitre on this corner turning to the left, work the yarnover and the following stitch with a left-slanting decrease, slip-slip-knit, as the row lengths progressively increase again.

◁ Cabled short-row mitre

Once you understand the principles of short rows, you can apply any pattern to the corner. Starting on a swatch, work the mitre corner and, at the same time, work each stitch as if the pattern was correct. If this doesn't look right, try to have major elements of the design, such as a cable, just before and immediately after the short rows, as in the swatch here. The third option is to design a complementary corner design, taking only elements of the edgings such as bobbles and using them as the short rows allow.

△ Textured short-row mitre with yarnovers

As the row length increases, work the yarnovers together with the following stitches with a right-slanting decrease, knit two together, to create a slight texture along the mitre.

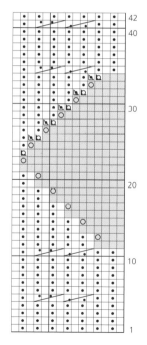

▷ Cabled short-row mitre chart

The drawn fabric created by this rib means that fewer short rows are required than would be expected for this number of stitches. The frequency of short rows and the number of stitches worked each short row can be calculated by looking at a gauge swatch and counting the number of rows that equal the width of the edging. This is the number of short rows required and can be divided into the number of stitches to calculate the number of stitches less that need to be worked for each alternate short row.

TIPS

If after knitting a sample mitred corner swatch a corner seems too tight and not quite square, try again with a needle size larger.

To create a knitted inwards-facing corner on an irregular-shaped blanket, work decreases instead of increases at the same frequency.

If you are knitting a corner that is not a right angle, a useful trick is to work two strips with no shaping and then attach them to the edge. Pinch and pin the strips together to form the perfect corner – letting the excess fabric hang free. Then count and note the stitches visible on each row before the corner seam – estimating any half stitches. A frequency of increases for an outside corner or decreases for a inside corner should become evident.

POMPOMS, TASSELS AND FRINGES

Pompoms, tassels and fringes are not just a fun indulgence, but are also an excellent way of improving the drape of a blanket.

Pompoms, tassels and fringes are yarn hungry and if the notion of adding such a trimming is at the back of your mind from the start, buy extra yarn. How much extra will depend on the thickness and length of the fringe or tassel, or the density, size and number of the pompoms. As soon as you can, make a sample trimming, noting how it was made and its weight. Multiply the weight of the trimming by its frequency to calculate how much yarn you will need.

If you have insufficient yarn, you will need to buy more, even if it is a different dye lot. The different texture of the trimming will disguise slight colour variations. The second option is to consider buying a contrasting or neutral-coloured yarn and mixing it in with any remaining yarn from the blanket. The third solution is to buy yarn that contrasts in texture or colour, and make the trimming a focal point of the blanket.

Trimmings are often an afterthought. With a completed blanket it is easier to see how it drapes and assess the finishing touches. However, where possible, you should plan in advance for every eventuality because yarns and colours are discontinued every season, and the option of matching yarns slips away.

MAKING A POMPOM

Clutches of pompoms at the corners or single pompoms attached along a blanket edge add weight and an element of fun. However, they are not suitable on blankets for small children as they are made up of short threads that are fairly easy to pull out.

There are many brands of pompom makers on the market, but the easiest method is to use two doughnut-shaped circles of cardboard. Start by determining the size of the pompom, then, if you are using DK-weight yarn, draw two circles about 10 per cent larger than the diameter desired. (This extra 10 per cent is for tidying and trimming the ball into shape at the end.) If you are using a lighter weight yarn, reduce this margin; if you are using a heavier weight yarn, increase it. Draw two smaller circles inside the first two circles. (The larger these holes are, the denser the pompom; the smaller the holes, the looser the pompom and the more likely it is to be slightly oval.) A good, medium-sized pompom is achieved with a second circle half the diameter of the finished pompom size.

1 Cut out the doughnut shapes from the cardboard and, holding them together, wind the yarn around the cardboard, working from inside the hole, around the cardboard, and back through the hole, each new wrap lying next to the last. Continue until the centre hole is filled, threading a needle with the yarn for the last wraps.

2 Using a pair of sharp scissors and cutting a few strands at a time, cut around the pompom edge between the two discs. Pry the discs slightly apart and tie a length of yarn tightly around the centre of the pompom. Remove the disks – it may be necessary to cut them. Tousle the yarn strands and trim the pompom to make a neat ball.

MAKING A TASSEL

Making a long, thick, lush tassel requires a lot of yarn, but often shorter tassels fit the proportion of a blanket better. The idea is not to simulate a horse's tail or to be endlessly trying to comb them out with your fingers. However, one trick for bulking out a tassel is to use yarn that is slightly fluffy and certainly to avoid smooth cotton or bamboo yarns.

Start by cutting a piece of cardboard the depth of the desired tassel. It does not have to be very wide and need not be very thick – just solid enough not to buckle as the yarn is wrapped round it.

2 Thread a second length of yarn through a needle. Pass this under the wrapped yarn and tie it around the tassel at the top edge of the cardboard. Cut the tassel along the bottom edge and remove the yarn. The start and end of the wrapped yarn will hang slightly lower. Trim the "skirt".

1 Hold the end of a length of yarn with your thumb halfway up the length of cardboard and wrap the yarn around the cardboard by moving down to the bottom of the cardboard, around the top, over the top, and back again. Continue until you reach the desired tassel thickness, and stop at the bottom of the cardboard, leaving 2.5 cm (1 in) free. Note the number of wraps.

3 Pass the second length of yarn threaded through the needle down through the tassel to the base of the desired tassel head. Wrap the yarn around the tassel once and pass the needle behind and over the start of the wrap. Wrapping in the opposite direction, wrap the tassel as many times as desired and secure the end.

◁ **Pompom tassel**
Sometimes the head of a tassel can seem rather flat. For this tassel, the skirt at the end of Step 2 (above) was used to secure a pompom.

◁ **Padded tassel**
Wadding is inserted in the centre of the top of the skirt, below the securing knot, before the tassel head is finished. This wadding provides a secure base for embellishment as well as altering the tassel head shape.

MAKING A FRINGE

Fringes are an excellent way of giving life to a blanket. They can be tamed by knotting them or weighing them slightly with beads. In all cases, fringes move with the blanket, creating new shapes and edges. Experiment with fluffy or bulky yarns, many or single yarns, and the spacing along the edge to create different effects. Note that too many fringes attached along an edge can cause the edge to splay and ripple slightly. This distance will vary from fabric to fabric, and from fringe yarn to fringe yarn.

Start by cutting a piece of cardboard twice the depth of the desired fringe. Wrap the yarn around the cardboard, then cut the yarn along both edges to create yarn lengths double the depth of the fringe.

Using a crochet hook, insert the hook through a stitch or space between two stitches on the edge to be fringed, either from front to back or back to front. Fold a length of cut yarn in half and loop the fold over the crochet hook. Draw the crochet hook and the loop of yarn through the edge, place the yarn ends over the hook, and draw through the first loop to knot in place. Continue to work along the edge. For an even fringe, work either front to back or back to front in each case and with equal spacing.

STITCH DIRECTORY

●

This section features a collection
of exciting stitch patterns and
motifs for knit and crochet.
Samples are coded by skill level
so beginners can choose easy
stitch patterns and more
experienced knitters and
crocheters can select more
challenging ones.

See page 6 for a key to the symbols used.

HOW TO READ A CHART

To read a chart, start at the bottom right and read odd-numbered rows (right side rows) from right to left and even-numbered rows (wrong side rows) from left to right (see page 26).

NOT A TARTAN

This design may not be the star of an blanket, but the technique is a useful way of creating a block that combines colours from other blocks in the blanket, so helping to unify the overall design. As three of the colours appear only in small quantities, any colour mix will work – the more the better.

For a 15-cm (6-in) square block using a DK-weight yarn:
Using yarn A, cast on 34 sts plus any selvedge sts using the thumb method.
Cont to work from the chart but work the yellow and red stitches indicated in the same colour as the previous stitch.
Rep charts rows until the charted rows have been completed or the block measures 15cm (6in) from the cast-on edge.
Cast off.
Stitch the yellow vertical stripes indicated by working surface crochet into every second stitch.
Stitch the red vertical stripes indicated by working duplicate stitch over every stitch.

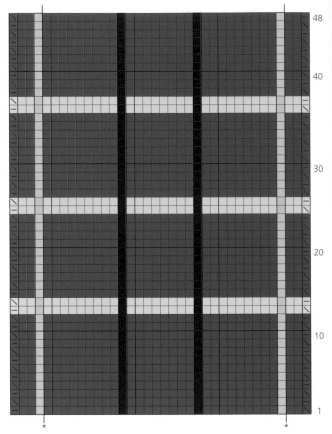

Colours: blue-green (A), lilac (B), yellow (C) and red (D)
Repeat: 34 sts plus selvedge sts

SEE ALSO

For the key to all symbols and abbreviations, see pages 134–135.

STRANDED

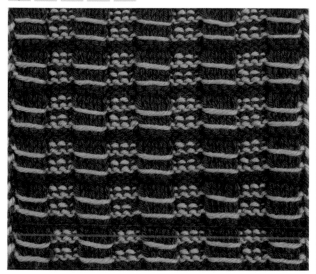

This is another stripe block variation. The second colour could be changed for many colours and the block could be worked on larger needles for an all-in-one blanket design.

For a 15-cm (6-in) square block using a DK-weight yarn:
Using yarn A, cast on 36 sts plus any selvedge sts using the thumb method.
Cont to work from the chart.
Rep chart rows until the block measures 15cm (6in) from the cast-on edge.
Cast off.

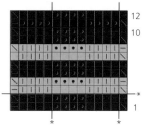

Colours: mulberry (A) and gold (B)
Repeat: 8 sts plus 4 sts plus selvedge sts

FAIR ISLE DUPLICITY

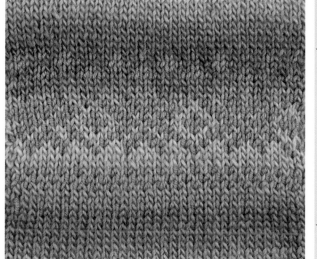

This is a case of something for nothing – the something is a lot of colour, the nothing is fewer ends that add bulk to an blanket seam. This is an easy pattern to memorize with large sections of stocking stitch to relieve the pressure of keeping the strands on the reverse even and neat. The strands are quite short, so should not pose too much of a snagging hazard.

For a 15-cm (6-in) square block using a DK-weight yarn:
Using yarn A, cast on 36 sts plus any selvedge sts using the thumb method.
Work 12 rows of stocking stitch.
Cont to work from the chart.
Work 12 rows of stocking stitch.
Bind off.

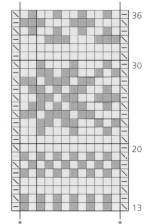

Colours: variegated yarn (A) and pink (B)
Repeat: 12 sts plus selvedge sts

FAIR ISLE REPEATS

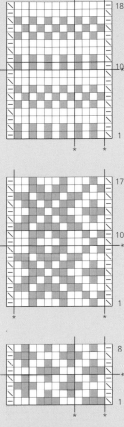

The individual stitch patterns used in Fair Isle Duplicity look good repeated. Consider these as options for other blocks in the blanket.

TIP

To avoid intarsia work looking uneven, work the reverse stocking stitch rows using a slightly smaller needle. This produces a row of smaller stitches, to which yarn from any baggy stitches on rows either side can be eased.

TIP

The reverse of the Knitted Ridges block is interesting and is almost a second block design for free. Alternate with front-facing and back-facing blocks to make the blanket reversible.

SEE ALSO

For the key to all symbols and abbreviations, see pages 134–135.

KNITTED RIDGES

The ridges of reverse stocking stitch in this pattern partially obscure the stocking stitches in the contrast colour between. So, more or less of the contrast colour is revealed as the fabric is handled. This stitch looks best if worked to a fairly tight tension.

For a 7.5-cm (3-in) square block using a DK-weight yarn:
Using yarn A, cast on 38 sts plus any selvedge sts using the thumb method.

Row 1: k16 sts, ssk, place marker, k2tog, k to the end of the row (36 sts).
Cont to work from the chart. Fasten off.
Repeat 3 more times to make enough blocks for a 15-cm (6-in) square block.
Seam the blocks together experimenting with the orientation of the blocks before doing so.

For a 15-cm (6-in) square block using a DK-weight yarn:
Using yarn A, cast on 76 sts plus any selvedge sts using the thumb method.
Row 1: k36 sts, ssk, place marker, k2tog, k to the end of the row (74 sts).
Cont to work the patt set in the chart until no sts remain.
Fasten off.

Colours: blue (A) and grey (B).

TUMBLING BLOCKS

This looks like a serious piece of intarsia work, but the repeat and shapes are simple to remember and the straight, diagonal lines make the edges easy to keep neat. Based on a popular patchwork motif, it is an excellent framework for using up yarn oddments. Let rip and use textured, shiny or variegated yarn; this design can take it all. It can also be worked in double crochet without adapting it. Chain the repeat plus 1 ch and work the first double crochet stitch in the 3rd ch from the hook.

For a 15-cm (6-in) square block using a DK-weight yarn:
Using yarn A, cast on 40 sts plus any selvedge sts using the thumb method. Cont to work from the chart. The stitches highlighted in blue are worked in oddments of yarn (see the photograph above).
Rep chart rows until the block measures 15cm (6in) from the cast-on edge.
Cast off.

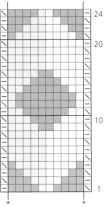

Colours: light grey (A) and dark grey (B), plus small amounts of many colours.
Repeat: 10 sts plus selvedge sts

HEARTS AND DOVES

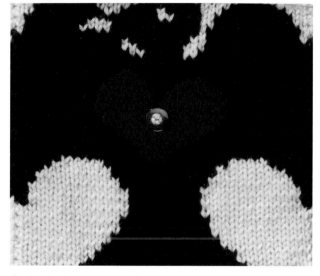

The inspiration for this block came when the negative space around a heart pattern on some giftwrap became apparent. This motif comes into its own when tiled with itself (see diagram, below right). In the example shown above, the heart in the centre has been made by knitting the heart motif separately, felting it and stitching it to the block, with a button for added decoration. (For the felted heart pattern, see above right.) For the complete knitted block in another colourway, see Choosing colours, page 24.

For a 15-cm (6-in) square block using a DK-weight yarn:
Using yarn A, cast on 34 sts plus any selvedge sts using the thumb method. Cont to work from the chart, working the centre heart in either yarn A or yarn B as shown above, until all the charted rows have been completed.
Cast off.

Colours: light grey (A), dark blue (B) and red (C).
Repeat: 34 sts plus selvedge sts

TIP

If necessary, use a fine cable needle to ease the stitches in the colour blocks into order. Start with the first stitch of an untidy section and ease the stitch loops, one side at a time, in the direction they were worked until the block is tidy.

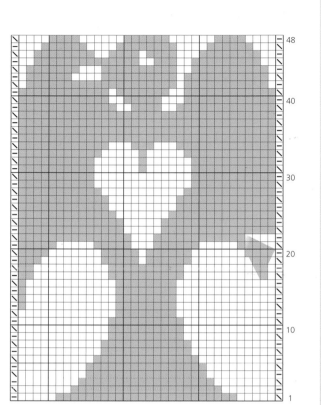

FELTED HEART

For the best results, yarn C must be 100 per cent wool. Using two strands of yarn C, cast on 3 sts using the thumb method.
The heart shape, based on the chart of the Hearts and Doves (left), is worked as follows:

Row 21: knit.
Row 22: inc in the first st, k1, inc in the last st (5 sts).
Row 23: knit.
Row 24: inc in the first st, k3, inc in the last st (7 sts).
Row 25: inc in the first st, k5, inc in the last st (9 sts).
Row 26: knit.
Row 27: inc in the first st, k7, inc in the last st (11 sts).
Row 28: inc in the first st, k9, inc in the last st (13 sts).
Row 29: knit.
Row 30: knit.
Row 31: k6, transfer the remaining stitches on the left-hand needle onto a stitch holder.
Row 32: knit.
Row 33: ssk, k4.
Row 34: ssk, k1, k2tog.
Cast off.
Cut yarn 4In (10cm) from the last stitch.
Transfer the stitches on the stitch holder to a needle and rejoin yarn.
Row 31: cast off the first stitch, k6.
Row 32: knit.
Row 33: k4, k2tog.
Row 34: ssk, k1, k2tog.
Cast off.
To felt the heart, put it in a small drawstring bag, add to a boil wash and then reshape before allowing it to dry.

SPITS AND SPOTS

Anything with bobbles can become a multi-coloured delight. For a coloured bobble, work the stitch below a bobble in a contrasting colour, then on the next row, use the same yarn to work the bobble and on the following row work the bobble stitch in the main colour again. In the lower photograph, the yarn tails from the coloured bobbles have not been woven in, but knotted and left on display.

KEY

■ Make bobble: [k into the front and back] six times into the st, pass the 2nd, 3rd, 4th and 5th sts on the right needle over the first and off the needle.

HORIZONTAL AND VERTICAL RIDGES

This stitch pattern is a good basic pattern on which to apply other embellishments, such as beads or yarnovers, and decreases instead of the bobbles. The blue highlight shows how the pattern is constructed. Extending or shortening the repeat works well, as do vertical intarsia stripes or horizontal stripes. The bobble shown is a no-turn bobble, which is useful if working on an all-in-one blanket.

For a 15-cm (6-in) square block using a DK-weight yarn:
Cast on 35 sts plus any selvedge sts using the thumb method.
Cont to work from the chart.
Rep chart rows until the block measures 15cm (6in) from the cast-on edge.
Cast off.

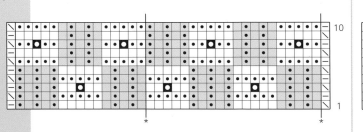

Repeat: 10 sts plus 5 sts plus selvedge sts

DIMPLE

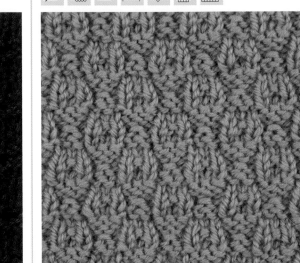

The stitch pattern repeat on this block is so small that it becomes almost imperceptible, and the block becomes just an interesting texture. Of course, the repeat can be enlarged, which would produce a lovely contrast if the blocks appeared together in the same blanket.

For a 15-cm (6-in) square block using a DK-weight yarn:
Cast on 36 sts plus any selvedge sts using the thumb method.
Cont to work from the chart.
Rep chart rows until the block measures 15cm (6in) from the cast-on edge.
Cast off.

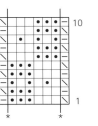

Repeat: 6 sts plus selvedge sts

DOUBLE CROSS

This pattern is a reversible rib pattern with a cable. Cables are not always reversible. However, in this repeat the cable row is repeated one row later on the reverse, and the reverse of the cables become part of the purl stitch repeat.

For a 15-cm (6-in) square block using a DK-weight yarn:
Cast on 40 sts plus any selvedge sts using the thumb method
Cont to work from the chart.
Rep chart rows until the block measures 15cm (6in) from the cast-on edge.
Cast off.

Repeat: 8 sts plus selvedge sts

VERTICAL TUCKS

The drape of this fabric is heavy when worked on needles close to those recommended for a yarn weight, but the fabric displays a different dominant colour on the right side from that on the reverse. This is the perfect stitch pattern for horizontal stripes, varying either the A colour or both the A and B colours. It is yarn hungry and progress is slower than that of patterns with fewer slipped stitches.

For a 15-cm (6-in) square block using a DK-weight yarn:
Using yarn A, cast on 46 sts plus any selvedge sts using the thumb method.
Cont to work from the chart.
Rep chart rows until the block measures 15cm (6in) from the cast-on edge.
Cast off.

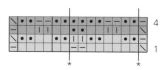

Colours: grey (A) and pink (B).
Repeat: 8 sts plus 6 sts plus selvedge sts

VERTICAL TUCKS ON THE REVERSE

A different colour dominates on each of the two faces of the fabric.

KEY

 Cable 2 back, slip the next st onto a cable needle and hold at the back of the work, k1, transfer the stitch from the cable needle back onto the left-hand needle, k1. Or without a cable needle: K into the front of the 2nd st on the left-hand needle and then k into the back of the first stitch, slipping both stitches off the needle at the same time.

Cable 2 forwards, slip the next st onto a cable needle and hold at the front of the work, k1, transfer the stitch from the cable needle back onto the left-hand needle, k1. Or without a cable needle: k into the back of the 2nd st on the left-hand needle and then k into the front of the first stitch, slipping both stitches off the needle.

KEY

Twist 5 back, slip the next 2 sts onto a cable needle and hold at the back of the work, k3, transfer the stitches from the cable needle back onto the left-hand needle, p1, k1.

Twist 5 forwards, slip the next 3 sts onto a cable needle and hold at the front of the work, k1, p1, transfer the stitches from the cable needle back onto the left-hand needle, k3.

Twist 5 forwards, slip the next 3 sts onto a cable needle and hold at the front of the work, p1, k1, transfer the stitches from the cable needle back onto the left-hand needle, k3.

Twist 5 back, slip the next 2 sts onto a cable needle and hold at the back of the work, k3, transfer the stitches from the cable needle back onto the left-hand needle, k1, p1.

SEE ALSO

For the key to all symbols and abbreviations, see pages 134–135.

CABLE CHEQUERS

The stitch repeat to make a reversible pattern is high but, as you can see from the highlighted area, the stitches within a repeat form two columns of eleven stitches, so stitches can be added, removed, or the repeat split into sections. The fabric may no longer be reversible, but it will still be attractive on both sides.

For a 15-cm (6-in) square block using a DK-weight yarn:
Cast on 50 sts plus any selvedge sts using the thumb method.
Cont to work from the chart.
Rep chart rows until the block measures 15cm (6in) from the cast-on edge.
Cast off.

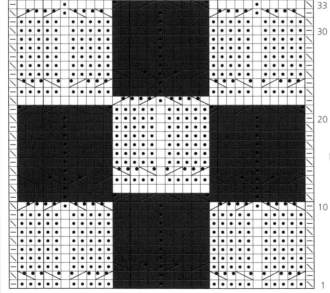

Repeat: 22 sts plus 6 sts plus selvedge sts

ADAPTED GUERNSEY

Traditional Guernsey knitting patterns explore texture, and in particular the textural possibilities of knit and purl stitches. These are also a good source of inspiration for lace designs. The geometric patterns have been worked out and it is just a matter of replacing the reverse stocking stitches with yarnovers, placing the decreases and adding a row of stocking stitch after each pattern row. Without the extra row, the fabric would be more lacy and the motif less distinct.

The lace pattern panel created from the seed stitch column of stitches in the original pattern is particularly useful as a background texture when worked over a greater number of stitches and on larger needles. It produces a light, easy-to-work fabric that is quick to produce. This is true of any lace pattern, but with some the detail of the design and its delicate nature would require careful handling and blocking to maintain the look. This makes some lace patterns more suitable for a shawl than a blanket, but the solution may be to add a row of knit or purl stitches between the existing pattern rows.

Note: Only odd-numbered rows are shown on the chart. For all even-numbered rows, purl.

For a 15-cm (6-in) square block using a DK-weight yarn:
Cast on 35 sts plus any selvedge sts using the thumb method.
Cont to work from the chart.
Rep chart rows until the block measures 15cm (6in) from the cast-on edge.
Cast off.

Repeat: 35 sts plus selvedge sts

GUERNSEY PATTERN VARIATIONS

This swatch was worked by translating the yarnovers in the Guernsey lace block chart (left) into reverse stocking stitches and not working the decreases in the pattern. The texture would be too subtle if the even-numbered rows were worked so that just the odd-numbered rows were worked back and forth across the swatch. Two repeats are required for a 15-cm (6-in) square block. Both lace and traditional Guernsey blocks could be worked in the same blanket to help unify the design.

LINKED BLOCKS

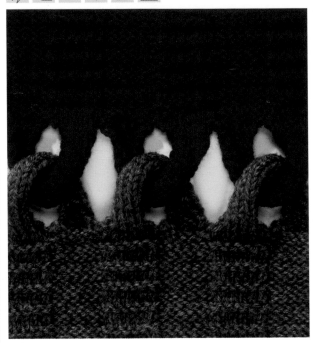

Colours: grey (A) and red (B).
Repeat: 6sts

Here is another idea to spark off others. The linked loops make sense in an blanket block because they create a light drape but also provide warmth and comfort, as well as being fun to make. Work in strong neutral colours for a modern, structured look, or in a mixture of bright colours to reflect its inherent sense of fun.

For a 15-cm (6-in) square block using a DK-weight yarn:
**Using yarn A, cast on 6 sts using a provisional cast on.
Row 1: knit.
Row 2 (WS): k1, p to the last st, k1.
Rep the last 2 rows until the block measures 7.5 cm (3 in) from the cast-on edge ending with a WS row.
Cut yarn 10 cm (4 in) from the needle but do not bind off.
Rep twice more.

Joining the strips
Starting with the last completed 7.5-cm (3-in) strip:
Row 1: k5, inc, undo the provisional cast on at its start, pick up the sts, and twist the strip clockwise so the wrong side is facing.
Sl the last st from the right-hand needle to the left-hand needle, k2tog, p4, inc, with the next 7.5-cm (3-in) strip on the left-hand needle, sl the last st from the right-hand needle to the left-hand needle, k2tog, *k4, inc, undo the provisional cast on at its start, pick up the sts, and twist the strip clockwise so the wrong side is facing.
Sl the last st from the right-hand needle to the left-hand needle, k2tog, p4, inc, with the next 7.5-cm (3-in) strip on the left-hand needle, sl the last st from the right-hand needle to the left-hand needle, k2tog, rep from * once more, k1.
Cont to work from the chart.
Rep chart's rows until the block measures 5cm (2in) from the base of the loops.
Do not bind off. Place sts on a spare needle.**
Rep from ** to ** in yarn B, looping each strip of fabric through a loop of fabric in yarn A, before purling the stitches at the base of the strip.
Cont to work from the chart, working an equal number of rows on each edge of live stitches until the block measures 15cm (6in).
Cast off both edges.

RUNNING LADDERS

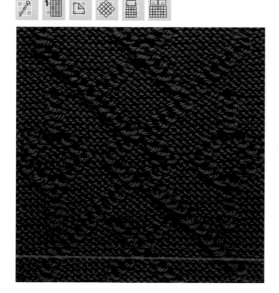

There is a naughty appeal to dropping stitches that is hard to beat. This pattern not only has stitches that are dropped, but they take a journey across and up the block. Ladders are started in the middle of a block with a yarnover and completed with another yarnover to keep the stitch count correct. Work this block to understand the method and use this technique to mirror the design of other blocks in an blanket or to reproduce your favourite travelling stitch designs. The reverse stocking stitch on the even-numbered rows acts as a marker to the stitches to be dropped, and reduces the amount of counting required on the reversible garter stitch background fabric.

For a 15-cm (6-in) square block using a DK-weight yarn:
Cast on 37 sts plus any selvedge sts using the thumb method.
Cont to work from the chart.
Rep chart rows until the block measures 15cm (6in) from the cast-on edge.
Bind off.

Repeat: 37 sts plus selvedge sts

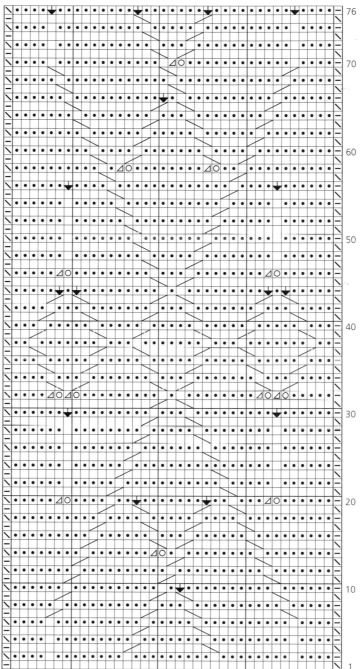

HOW TO READ A CHART

To read a chart, start at the bottom right and read odd-numbered rows (right side rows) from right to left and even-numbered rows (wrong side rows) from left to right. To each repeat total, add stitches to the foundation chain for the turning chain. This turning chain is also the first stitch.

SEE ALSO

For the key to all symbols and abbreviations, see pages 134–135.

FILET FROM A CORNER

The beauty of this pattern is that it is worked from the corner out, so it is easy to adjust the size to that required. Use the filet mesh stitch pattern to create filet motifs with the same advantage.

For a 15-cm (6-in) square block using a DK-weight yarn:
Foundation chain: using yarn A, make a slip knot.
Row 1: ch 3 (counts as 1 tr), tr 3 times into the slip knot (4 sts). Turn.
Cont to work from the chart, then cont to work the pattern set in the last row charted until the block measures 15cm (6in) from the foundation chain.
Fasten off yarn.

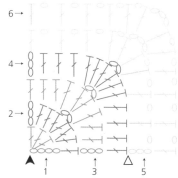

Colours: blue (A) and grey (B).

WOVEN STRIPS

This block idea will help to use up your stash of odd balls. Any kind of strip, approximately 5cm (2in) wide and 12.5cm (5in) long, can be used in the same way, whether crochet or knitted. In the solid double crochet shown here, it does have a heavy drape, but this could be eased with a different stitch pattern. This is an idea to experiment with.

For a 15-cm (6-in) square block using a DK-weight yarn:

STRIP
Foundation chain: using yarn A, ch 10.
Row 1: yo, insert the hook into the 4th ch from the hook, work 1 tr. This completes the first 2 sts. 1tr into each ch to the end of the row- (8 sts). Turn.
Row 2: ch 3 (counts as 1 tr), 1 tr into each st to the end of the row, work the last tr into the 2nd ch of the beg-ch before turning.
Rep row 2 until the strip measures 12.5cm (5in) from the foundation chain.
Fasten off yarn.
Rep once more in yarn A.
Rep twice in yarn B.
Rep twice in yarn C.

BLOCK
Weave the strips over and under as shown in the photograph and pin in place.
Using yarn D and the sts at the top and bottom of the strips as a guide, insert the hook through the two layers of each fabric and join in the yarn.
Edging: ch 3 (counts as 1 tr), 1 tr into each st to the end of the edge, ch 3, rep from * to the end of the rnd, join with a sl st into the top of the beg-ch.
Fasten off yarn.

VERTICAL DASHES

This stitch pattern is about the technique rather than the arrangement that is shown here. Working in strands can unify a design by using yarns from another block, and it uses up small scraps of yarn, and is reversible if the wrong side row is a repeat of the right side row. The base is simple: treble crochet into each stitch; the background fabric should be quite sturdy.

For a 15-cm (6-in) square block using a DK-weight yarn:
Foundation chain: ch 31.
Row 1: yo, insert the hook into the 4th ch from the hook, work 1 tr. This completes the first 2 sts. Cont to work from the chart to the end of the row (29 sts).
Ch 3 (counts as 1 tr) at the beginning of each row, and work the last tr into the 2nd ch of the beg-ch before turning.
Cont to work from the chart.
Rep chart rows until the block measures 15cm (6in) from the foundation chain.
Fasten off yarn.

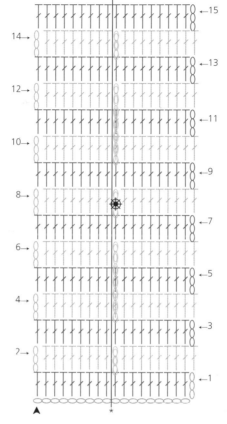

Colours: blue (A) and yellow (B).
Repeat: 10 sts plus 9 sts

KEY

Fold an 8-in (20-cm) length of yarn B in half, insert the hook fp around the st indicated, draw the center of the fold of yarn B through, ch the number of ch indicated with the two strands of yarn B, yarn A yo, draw through last ch of yarn B and last st lp of yarn A. On foll row this last ch is worked as a st.

Place bead on the ch of yarn B before working the last yo of yarn A.

RADIATING SPOTS

Crochet can be very heavy unless it is worked using an open stitch, but then this does not always provide the comfort of a solid knit blanket. One of the solutions is to choose a block shape that does not tessellate perfectly, so that you achieve a solid fabric feel as well as a cosseting drape. For a filler motif between 15-cm (6-in) circular blocks, work only the first three rounds of the block pattern and join the blocks together with slip stitches into neighbouring blocks on the last round.

For a 15-cm (6-in) block using a DK-weight yarn:
Foundation chain: using yarn A, make a slip knot.
Rnd 1: ch 3 (counts as 1 tr), tr 11 times into the slip knot (12 sts).
Cont to work from the chart.
If necessary, work rnds of the inc pattern set in yarn B until it measures 15cm (6in) from the foundation chain.
Fasten off yarn.

DEALING WITH LOOSE ENDS

To avoid unslightly strands of yarns between blocks of colour, weave the colour not being used into the yarn of the stitch being worked. Insert the hook into the next st, yo, draw the yarn through, wrap the yarn not being worked round the hook from below, wrap the yarn being worked round the hook in the same direction, take the yarn not being worked back to the back of the work. Using the yarn on the hook, complete the double crochet stitch. This traps the yarn not being worked into the stitch being worked. Repeat this process for every stitch.

Colours: brown (A) and cream (B).

HEXAGON WITH CIRCLES

This block combines two of the most versatile shapes. The hexagon will tessellate to form a solid fabric, and the circle motif is easily adapted to many other stitch pattern designs.

For a 15-cm (6-in) square block using a DK-weight yarn:
Foundation chain: using yarn A, make a slip knot.
Rnd 1: ch 3 (counts as 1 tr), tr 11 times into the slip knot (12 sts).
Cont to work from the chart.
If necessary, work rnds of the inc pattern set in yarns A and B, until it measures 12.5cm (5in) from the foundation chain. Divide the number of sts by six and work the rep (12 sts on the chart below) for each hexagon edge with the additional sts worked in single crochet in the middle of the rep.
Fasten off yarn.

Colours: pink (A), red (B), light blue (C) and blue (D).

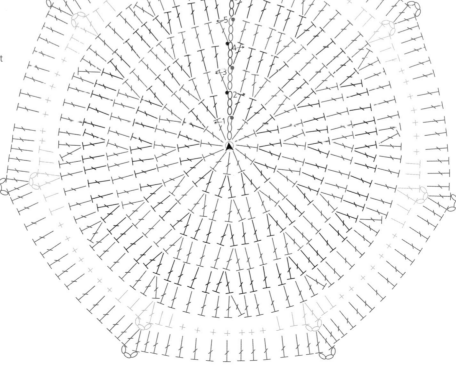

SEE ALSO

For the key to all symbols and abbreviations, see pages 134–135.

BASKETWEAVE

Raised stitch patterns
such as basketweave work
well in yarns that fade or
wear, such as some denim
yarns. They also create a
lush depth in soft yarns
like chenille or mohair.

SEE ALSO

For the key to all symbols
and abbreviations, see
pages 134–135.

TWO-COLOUR BASKETWEAVE

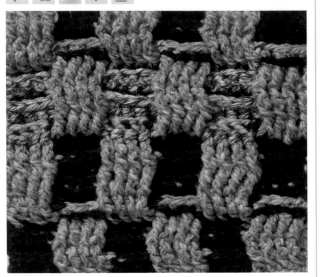

The joy of this stitch pattern is its appearance on both the right
and the wrong side. Although both the main and the contrast
colour are visible on both sides, one is more dominant than the
other on each. The fabric is too dense for large areas, but a
lighter drape can be achieved by using a taller stitch.

For a 15-cm (6-in) square block using a DK-weight yarn:
Foundation chain: using yarn A, ch 28.
Row 1: yo, insert the hook into the 4th ch from the hook, work
1 tr. This completes the first 2 sts. Cont to work from the chart
to the end of the row (26 sts).
Ch 3 (counts as 1 tr) at the beginning
of each row, and work the last tr
into the 2nd ch of the beg-ch
before turning.
Cont to work from the chart.
Rep chart rows until the block
measures 15cm (6in) from the
foundation chain.
Fasten off yarn.

Colours: blue (A), orange (B) and light
brown (C).
Repeat: 8 sts plus 2 sts

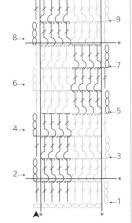

MOVING BLOCKS

The structure of this block is like a floating bridge and is
adaptable to any number of stitch patterns. It can appear as a
single block or the smaller blocks can continue to be added to
create an all-in-one blanket.

For a 15-cm (6-in) square block using a DK-weight yarn:
Foundation chain: using yarn A, ch 18.
Row 1: yo, insert the hook into the 4th ch from the hook, work
1 tr. This completes the first 2 sts. Cont to work from the chart
to the end of the row (16 sts).
Ch 3 (counts as 1 tr) at the beginning of each row, and work the
last dc into the 2nd ch of the beg-ch before turning.
*Cont to work from the chart,
joining in yarn B for the final
ch indicated.
Rep from * until the fourth
rep, then join the edge of the
fourth block to that of the first
block with a sl st at the end of
the 4th and then the final row.
Fasten off yarn.

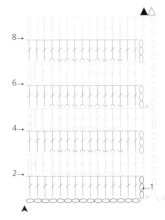

Colours: pink (A), burgundy (B),
chestnut (C) and brown (D).

TWISTED STRIPS

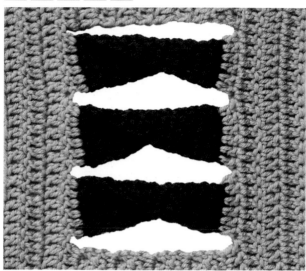

This block is ideal to help use up your stash of odd balls, but it does rely on neighbouring blocks to give it stability. Short strips could be used in an all-in-one blanket to great success.

Colours: purple (A) and lilac (B).

For a 15-cm (6-in) square block using a DK-weight yarn:

STRIP

Foundation chain: using yarn A, ch 8.
Row 1: yo, insert the hook into the 4th ch from the hook, work 1 tr. This completes the first 2 sts. 1 tr into each ch to the end of the row (6 sts). Turn.
Row 2: ch 3 (counts as 1 tr), 1 tr into each st to the end of the row, work the last tr into the 2nd ch of the beg-ch before turning.
Rep row 2 until the strip measures 7.5cm (3in) from the foundation chain.
Fasten off yarn.
Rep twice more in yarn A.
Rep twice in yarn B.

BLOCK

Position as shown in the photograph, with all the strips with the foundation ch lying in the same direction.
Using yarn B, join in the yarn into the top right st of one of the strips of yarn B
Row 1: ch 3 (counts as 1 tr), 1 tr into each st along the first and then the rem strips, to the end of the strips.

Row 2: ch 3 (counts as 1 tr), 1 tr into each st to the end of the row.
Rep the last row twice more. Do not fasten off yarn.
Turn the block so that the free ends of the strips are at the top ready to work. Starting with the strip on the far right, twist it 180 degrees anticlockwise, join in the yarn into the now top right st of the strip.
Row 1: ch 3 (counts as 1 tr), 1 tr into each st along the first and then the rem strips, rotating each in turn 180 degrees anticlockwise, to the end of the strips.
Row 2: ch 3 (counts as 1 tr), 1 tr into each st to the end of the row.
Rep the last row twice more. Do not fasten off yarn.
Check the depth of the block and work additional rows until the work measures 15cm (6in).
Fasten off yarn at both ends.

BROOMSTICK TUCKS

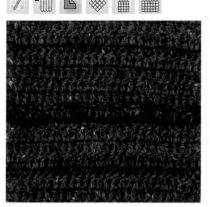

Broomstick tucks are lighter than the normal tuck, and the addition of a second strand of yarn in a stitch pattern is a useful idea to remember.

EQUIPME T

12.75mm (US17) knitting needle or a strip of card the depth of tuck required

ot : The first stitch placed onto the knitting needle is the last stitch loop of the row before extended to fit.

For a 15-cm (6-in) square block using a DK-weight yarn:
Foundation chain: ch 30.
Row 1: yo, insert the hook into the 4th ch from the hook, work 1 tr; this completes the first 2 sts. Cont to work from the chart to the end of the row (28 sts).
Ch 3 (counts as 1 tr) at the beginning of each row, and work the last tr into the 2nd ch of the beg-ch before turning.
Cont to work from the chart.
Rep chart rows until the block measures 15cm (6in) from the foundation chain.
Fasten off yarn.

Colours: blue (A), and main colour blue with an additional strand of mohair (B).
Repeat: 1 st

BROOMSTICK TUCKS WITHOUT THE TUCKS

The swatch above has been worked as the Broomstick Tucks swatch (left), but the double crochet tuck rows have not been worked. This produces stripes of longer yarn strands that improve the drape of the swatch.

KEY

Using the yarn indicated and working from left to right, insert the hook into the fl of the next st, yo, draw the yarn through, and place the lp onto the knitting needle or strip of cardboard.

RADIATING FILET MOTIF

The addition of more colours to any of the swatches will alter their appearance and the above swatch combines two swatches from the directory, Radiating Spots and Radiating Filet, to create this third swatch. The possibilities for adapting designs to this round filet grid are endless.

RADIATING FILET

This has been included because it is a wonderful framework on which to create your own designs. To make it into a square block, look at the block pattern on page 55.

For a 15-cm (6-in) block using a DK-weight yarn:
Foundation chain: using yarn A, make a slip knot.
Rnd 1: ch 3 (counts as 1 tr), tr 11 times into the slip knot (12 sts). Cont to work from the chart. If necessary, work rnds of the inc pattern set until it measures 15cm (6in) from the foundation chain. Fasten off yarn.

KEY

⊤ tr fp, around the last
⊥ st or ch worked.

FLOWER

For the single applied flower for the Filet Throw on page 131, work as described here, but work 12 tr fp sts to create the petal.

For a 15-cm (6-in) square block using a DK-weight yarn:
Foundation chain: using yarn A, make a slip knot.
Rnd 1: ch 1 dc, 8 times into the slip knot (8 tr sts).
Cont to work from the chart.
Fasten off yarn.
Rep in yarn B, joining two petals to adjacent petals in the first flower.
Work one more flower in yarn A and one more flower in yarn B, and arrange as shown in the photograph.

Colours: pink (A) and blue (B).

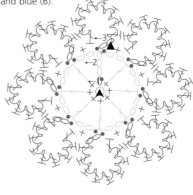

HOUNDSTOOTH

This block pattern has been included because of the technique it uses. Working a block blanket is the perfect time to learn new techniques because the pieces are small and easy to handle and it is always possible to change your mind about how many blocks you may need in the blanket. This colour technique produces a reversible colour pattern using the same strands of yarn several times in a row without the problem of making the strands of yarn neat on the following row.

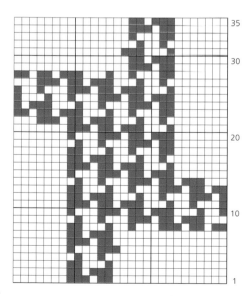

For a 15-cm (6-in) block using a DK-weight yarn:
Foundation chain: using yarn A, ch 29.
Row 1: insert the hook into the 3rd ch from the hook, work 1 dc. This completes the first 2 sts. Cont to work from the chart using dc to the end of the row (28 sts).
Ch 2 (counts as 1 dc) at the beginning of each row, and work the last dc into the bottom of the beg-ch before turning.
Cont to work from the chart.
Fasten off yarn.

Colours: green (A) and brown (B).
Repeat: 28 sts.

SCAFFOLDING

A small section of scaffolding outside the window inspired this simple geometric design. The straight lines and angles suit the limited capacity of an image created by a 15-cm (6-in) square block using DK-weight yarn.

For a 15-cm (6-in) square block using a DK-weight yarn:
Foundation chain: ch 35.
Row 1: yo, insert the hook into the 4th ch from the hook, work 1 tr, tr into the next ch. This completes the first mesh. Cont to the end of the row using the chart as reference and counting each ch as either a sp or a st. Turn.
Ch 3 (counts as 1 tr) at the beginning of each row, and work the last tr into the 2nd ch of the beg-ch before turning.
Cont to work from the chart.
Rep chart rows until the block measures 15cm (6in) from the foundation chain.
Fasten off yarn.

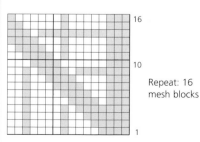

Repeat: 16 mesh blocks

REPEAT DESIGNS

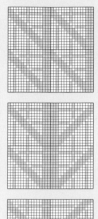

It is when the Scaffolding block (left) is repeated that it begins to hold its own, looking fresh and modern. Similar shapes are easy to find and the addition of beading, popcorns or appliqué can be used to relieve the flat texture.

KEY

Open mesh: ch 1, sk 1 sp or tr, tr into the next tr st.

Solid mesh: tr into the next sp or st, tr into the next tr st.

FLOWER AND FILET

CROCHET FLOWER

The addition of more colours to any of the swatches will alter their appearance and give them a different emphasis. The flower in this Flower and Filet swatch (right) can be worked separately and applied to other blanket s uares.

KEY

☐ **Open mesh:** ch 1, sk 1 sp or tr, tr into the next tr st.

☐ **Solid mesh:** tr into the next sp or st, tr into the next tr st.

This filet is worked in the round around a crochet flower. This technique can be adapted to any flower or similar shape, and the filet can be replaced by another filet or crochet design.

ot : Each corner space counts as 5 stitches, spaces, or chains.

FLOWER

Foundation chain: make a slip knot.
Rnd 1: ch 5 (counts as 1 tr and 2 ch), tr and ch 2, 7 times into the slip knot (8 tr sts).
Rnd 2: *[dc, htr, tr, htr, dc] into the next sp), rep from * 7 times more, join with a sl st into the first dc, ch 3, turn.

Rnd 3: tr fp around the beg-ch of rnd 1. Working around the tr sts of the first rnd, * ch 4, tr fp around the next tr st, ch 1, tr fp around the next tr st, rep from * twice more, ch 4, tr fp around the next tr st, ch 1, join with a sl st into the first tr, turn.

FILET

Ch 3, starting with a corner. Work anticlockwise, following the chart.
Ch 3 (counts as 1 tr) at the beginning of each row, and work the last tr into the 2nd ch of the beg-ch before turning.
Cont to work from the chart.
If necessary, rep rows of solid mesh until the block measures 15cm (6in) from the foundation chain.
Fasten off yarn.

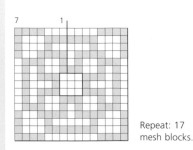

7   1

Repeat: 17 mesh blocks.

CONCENTRIC CIRCLES

This block demonstrates the idea of containing a motif within another motif. The inner ring can move freely within the chains in round two, which are worked around it. A blanket made up with many of these blocks will not look uniform and will have more movement. The inner ring can be substituted for a square shape, or found objects such as plastic rings or beads, but think about whether the finished blanket needs to provide comfort or is purely decorative. Choosing something too big or unyielding will distort the blanket.

For a 15-cm (6-in) square block using a DK-weight yarn:
INNER RING
Foundation chain: using yarn A, ch 36.
Rnd 1: ch 3 (counts as 1 tr), tr 53 times into the ring, join with a sl st into the beg-ch (54 sts).
Fasten off yarn.

MOTIF
Foundation chain: using yarn A, make a slip knot.
Rnd 1: ch 3 (counts as 1 tr), tr 11 times into the slip knot (12 sts).
Continue to work from the chart, working rnd 2 ch around the inner ring.
Fasten off yarn.

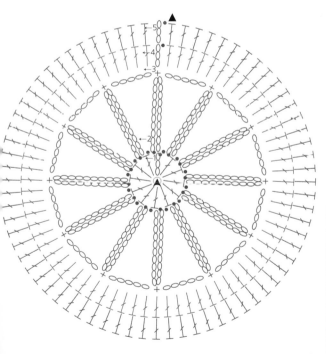

Colours: mustard (A) and old terracotta (B).

TESSELLATING CIRCLES

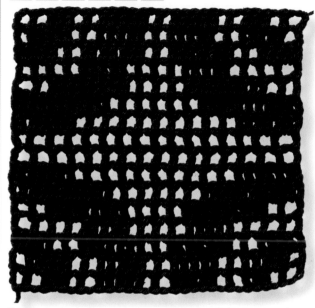

This block also looks good when repeated and then arranged together. Team it with any one of the circular motifs, add surface crochet to the centre, or appliqué crochet rings to add extra interest.

For a 15-cm (6-in) square block using a DK-weight yarn:
Foundation chain: ch 36.
Row 1: yo, insert the hook into the 6th ch from the hook, work 1 tr. This completes the first mesh. Cont to the end of the row using the chart as reference and counting each ch as either a sp or a st. Turn.
Ch 3 (counts as 1 tr) at the beginning of each row and work the last tr into the 2nd ch of the beg-ch before turning.
Cont to work from the chart.
Rep chart rows until the block measures 15cm (6in) from the foundation chain.
Fasten off yarn.

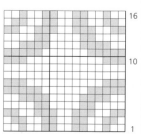

Repeat: 16 mesh blocks.

MIX AND MATCH

The Concentric Circles swatch (opposite) without the inner circle makes a good companion to the original swatch, or work just rounds one and two for a flower motif.

THE
PROJECTS

●

A collection of charming
projects to try out your
skills, from a Fair Isle
throw in rich autumn
shades to a delicate
cashmere bed throw in
filet crochet.

Finished size
Cushion one (right) 30 x 30cm
(12 x 12in)
Cushion two (left) 45 x 45cm
(18 x 18in)

Yarn
Front (for both cushions)
Rowan Calmer (80 per cent
cotton, 20 per cent Elite
polyester fibre; 160m [175yd]/
50g [1¾oz]), #492 Garnet (A):
1 ball; #479 Slosh (B): 1 ball;
#493 Plum (C): 1 ball.

Cushion one back
Rowan Calmer (80 per cent
cotton, 20 per cent Elite
polyester fibre; 160m [175yd]/
50g [1¾oz]), #492 Garnet (A):
3 balls.

Cushion two back
Rowan Calmer (80 per cent
cotton, 20 per cent Elite
polyester fibre; 160m [175yd]/
50g [1¾oz]), #492 Garnet (A):
1 ball; #479 Slosh (B): 1 ball;
#493 Plum (C): 2 balls.

Equipment
5.5mm (US9) knitting needles
4mm (USG-6) crochet hook
Cable needle (cn)
Tapestry needle

Notions
Buttons (2.5mm [1in]) waste
or cheap shank buttons to
cover: 5.

Techniques
Buttonholes
Cables

Tension
Knitting gauge
16 sts and 24 rows =
10 x 10cm (4 x 4in) in
stocking stitch.

Crochet block tension
One block =
15 x 15cm (6 x 6in)

CUSHION

There are magazine articles and podcasts devoted to the discussion of what to do with tension swatches or experiment blocks. One solution is a cushion cover. A well-loved cushion cover does not last forever, so a few spares are always welcome. The yarn used in this cushion is perfect. It holds a lot of air because of the two lengths of bonded strands plied together. It feels light, plush, and also has a warm, comforting touch.

Abbreviations

Knit

c2b cable 2 back, sl the next st onto the cn and hold at the back of the work, k1 from the left-hand needle, k1 from the cn.

c2f cable 2 forwards, sl the next st onto the cn and hold at the front of the work, k1 from the left-hand needle, k1 from the cn.

cr3f cross 3 forwards, sl the next 2 sts onto the cn and hold at the front of the work, k1 from the left-hand needle, sl the left st back onto the left-hand needle, p1, k1 from the cn.

k knit

p purl

sl slip

t2b twist 2 back, sl the next st onto the cn and hold at the back of the work, k1 from the left-hand needle, p1 from the cn.

t2f twist 2 forwards, sl the next st onto the cn and hold at the front of the work, p1 from the left-hand needle, k1 from the cn.

Crochet

ch chain

sl st slip stitch

tr treble crochet

CUSHION ONE FRONT

Block one

Work the log cabin block on page 72 as follows:

Work 2 rnds in yarn A.

Work ½ rnd (2 sides of the square) using yarn B, join in yarn C.

Work 1 rnd using yarn C, change to yarn B, work 1 rnd.

Rep from * to * once more.

Work 1 more rnd using yarn C, change to yarn B, work ½ rnd.

Fasten off.

Repeat twice more.

Block two

Work as for block one but start with 2 rnds of yarn C and complete the square swapping yarn A for yarn C in the sequence above.

Fasten off.

BACK

Lower back

This piece is worked from the top, open edge, down.

Work with two strands of yarn throughout. Using yarn A, cast on 63 sts using the cable cast-on method.

Row 1 (WS): k1tbl, k1, *p4, k7*, rep from * to * 4 more times, p4, k1, yfwd sl st purlwise.

Row 2: k1tbl, k1, *k4, p7*, rep from * to * 4 more times, k5, yfwd sl st purlwise.

Rep the last 2 rows until the work measures 30cm (12in) from the cast-on edge.

Cast off.

Back flap

This piece is worked from the bottom, open edge, up.

Work with two strands of yarn throughout. Using yarn A, cast on 63 sts using the cable cast-on method.

Row 1 (RS): k1tbl, k1, *p4, k7*, rep from * to * 4 more times, p4, k1, yfwd sl st purlwise.

Row 2 and all even-numbered rows: k1tbl, k1, k the k sts and p the p sts as presented along the row until the last 2 sts, k1 yfwd sl st purlwise.

Rep the last 2 rows until the work measures 2.5cm (1in) from the cast-on edge, ending with a WS row.

Buttonhole row: k1tbl, k1, *p4, k1, yfwd, sl1, yb, leave yarn to hang at the back of the work, [sl1, psso] 4 times more, pass last sl st back onto the left-hand needle, turn, pick up yarn and cast on 6 sts using the cable method, turn, sl 1st from the right-hand needle to the left-hand needle, k2tog*, rep from * to * 4 more times, p4, k1, yfwd sl st purlwise.

Cont in the rib pattern set until the work measures 1in (2.5cm) from the buttonhole row, ending with a WS row.

Next row: k1tbl, k1, *p4, foll chart sts*, rep from * to * 4 more times, p4, k1, yfwd sl st purlwise.

Rep the last row until the chart is completed, keeping the rib patt correct either side of the chart sts. Cont in the rib patt set until the work measures 15cm (6in) from the cast-on edge, ending with a WS row.

Cast off.

Cushion one back

The crochet buttons need not all be the same colour – in fact, odd ends of yarn or multi-coloured hand-dyed yarn can be used.

CUSHION TWO

This 45- x 45-cm (18- x 18-in) cushion back was worked using nine 15-cm (6-in) square crochet blocks for the lower back section, based on the log cabin block on page 72. For the back flap extra purl stitches were added to the purl section of the rib to increase the width. The buttons are made by working the first two rounds of the log cabin block and were finished as the buttons left.

Lower back
Block one
Work the log cabin block on page 72 as follows:
Work 2 rnds in yarn C.
Work ½ rnd (2 sides of the square) using yarn B, join in yarn A.
Work 1 rnd using yarn A, change to yarn B, work 1 rnd
Rep from * to * once more.
Work 1 more rnd using yarn A, change to yarn B, work ½ rnd.
Fasten off.
Repeat 7 times more.

Block two
Work as for block one but start with 2 rnds of yarn A and complete the square, swapping yarn C for yarn A in the sequence above.
Fasten off.

Back flap
The stitches that differ from those of the 30-cm (12-in) cushion are in bold type. These stitches are always worked as rev st st.
Using yarn C, cast on 81 sts using the cable cast-on method.
Row 1 (RS): k1tbl, k1, *p7, k7*, rep from * to * 4 more times, p7, k1, yfwd sl st purlwise.
Row 2 and all even numbered rows: k1tbl, k1, k the k sts and p the p sts as presented along the row, until the last 2 sts, k1 yfwd sl st purlwise.
Cont working as for main cushion with the increased number of reverse stocking stitches between the stocking stitches as viewed from the RS.

Cushion one front
The front can be worked using any 15-cm (6-in) square blocks. They can match or contrast with a blanket design.

Finishing
Block the pieces using the ball band as a guide.
Using the photograph as reference, lay out the front pieces so that the outer blue stitches are to the top and left and block two is to the bottom right.
Using yarn B and right sides facing outwards, slip stitch seam through the inner chain loops only, join the front blocks, working the horizontal and then the vertical seams.
With wrong sides together, pin the lower back and back flap to the front, noting that the two back sections have contrasting rib patterns.
Using yarn A, join using double crochet through the top loops of the two edges, working three double crochet stitches into the corner stitches until all the edges have been joined. Slip stitch into the top of the first seam stitch made, ch1 and reverse double crochet (crab stitch) back across all the edge double crochet seam stitches.
Fasten off.
Weave in and secure all the ends.

BUTTONS
Using yarn C, work the first two rounds of the chart on page 113.
Fasten off.
Rep 9 more times.

Finishing
Layer one disc with the right side facing down, one button with the shank of the button pushed through the hole in the centre of the first disc, and a second disc with the right side facing upwards.
Single crochet seam the two discs together.
Fasten off.
Weave in and secure all ends.
Secure to the lower back section of the cushion.

Finishing

Block the pieces using the ball band
as a guide.

Lay out the front pieces so that the outer red
stitches are to the top and right.

Using yarn C and right sides facing outwards,
slip stitch seam through the inner chain loops
only, join the front blocks, working the
horizontal and then the vertical seams.

Make the button by using yarn A, working the
first two rounds of the log cabin square on
page 72 and finishing as the buttons left.

Cushion two front

The front was worked in the same way
as block one of cushion one, but four
rounds were worked before the colour
change to yarn B. The front continued
in the pattern set until the block was
35cm (14in) along each edge. The
cushion front was completed using yarn
A along two sides, only until the block
was 45cm (18in) along each edge.

Cushion two back

Only the back flap was knitted – the lower
back is made of spare crochet blocks.

FAIR ISLE THROW

Combining a knitted fabric and a length of cloth to make a throw is not cheating; it is making the most of the fibres and techniques available to you. The knitted Fair Isle tube adds cosiness and visual interest to the throw, as well as hiding the vulnerable reverse-side stranding of Fair Isle. The fabric adds durability and a texture that complements the knitted fabric. It is quick and easy, practical and beautiful.

Any self-striping yarn will work well, but this yarn is particularly soft and light. It contrasts with the wool of the second colours.

Finished size
115 x 23cm (45 x 9in)

Yarn
Rowan Tapestry (70 per cent wool, 30 per cent soybean protein; 120m [131yd]/ 50g [1¾oz]), #171 Rainbow (A): 5 balls. Rowan Pure Wool DK (100 per cent wool; 125m [136yd]/ 50g [1¾oz]), #020 Parsley (B): 2 balls; #022 Emerald (C): 2 balls; #019 Avocado (D): 2 balls; #021 Glade (E): 2 balls.

Equipment
4mm (US6) 45cm (18in) circular knitting needle
4mm (USG-6) crochet hook
Tapestry needle

Notions
A length of fabric or a blanket 115cm (45in) wide to the required depth for the throw.

Techniques
Fair Isle

Tension
24 sts and 30 rows = 10 x 10cm (4 x 4in) in stocking stitch.

Abbreviations
Knit
k   knit
k2tog knit two together

Crochet
dc   double crochet

STRIP
This pattern is based on the Fair Isle Duplicity pattern on page 101.
Using yarn A, cast on 121 sts using the thumb method.
Prepare to join for working in the round, taking care not to twist the stitches. Slip the last cast-on st onto the left-hand needle, k2tog.

Rows 1–12: k.
Rows 13–39: work from the chart.
Rows 40–51: k.
Rows 52–60: work from the chart.
Rows 61–72: k.
Rows 73–99: work from the chart.
Rep from row 1 until the work measures 90cm (36in) from the cast-on edge.
Cast off.

FINISHING
Block the strip using the ball band as a guide with the round's start position along one edge.
Using yarn E, dc around the cast-on and bound-off edges and along the two fold edges of the knitted strip, inserting the hook round the stitch on the edge.
Hem the fabric if necessary and join to the knitted fabric to the cloth using whip stitch.
Weave in and secure all the ends.

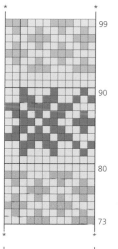
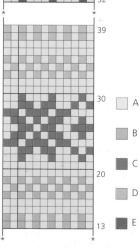

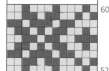

☐	A
▨	B
■	C
▨	D
■	E

SHRUG

The styling of this shrug is reminiscent of a kimono and has that same smart, casual look. The blocks can be swapped for any in the book, matching the firm tension of the knitted squares and the light drape of the crochet lace blocks. The yarn used has good stitch definition, with the subtle variegation in the main colour yarn adding some added interest to the fabric. The second green colour matches a fleck of colour in the main colour yarn.

Finished size
92cm (36in) from sleeve edge to sleeve edge

Yarn
Rowan Classic Yarns, Cotton Jeans (100 per cent cotton; 75m [82yd]/ 50g [1¾oz]), #366 Blue Jeans (A): 8 balls; Rowan Handknit Cotton (100 per cent cotton; 85m [93yd]/ 50g [1¾oz]), #219 Gooseberry (B): 3 balls.

Equipment
4mm (US6) knitting needles
5mm (USH-8) crochet hook
Tapestry needle

Techniques
Lace crochet

Tension
Block = 15 x 15cm (6 x 6in).
Adjust needle and hook size to achieve tension.

Abbreviations
Knit
k knit
k2tog knit two together
p purl
ssk slip, slip, knit two together on the right-hand needle by inserting left needle through the front of the loops

Crochet
ch chain
dc double crochet
tr treble crochet

BLOCKS

Two-tone blocks
Using yarn A, cast on 54 sts plus any selvedge sts using the thumb method.
Row 1 (WS): k25 sts, ssk, place marker, k2tog, k to the end of the row (52 sts).
Cont to work the patt set in the chart on page 74 until 8 sts rem.
On decrease rows, work the decreases before and after the stitch marker.
Knit every row, cont with dec as set until 2 sts remain.
Next row: k2tog.
Cast off.
Rep 3 times more; total: 4 blocks.

Three-stripe blocks
Using yarn A, cast on 54 sts plus any selvedge sts using the thumb method.
Row 1 (RS): k25 sts, ssk, place marker, k2tog, k to the end of the row (52 sts).
Cont to work the st patt as for the two-tone block with the foll yarn stripe sequence.
Rows 2–6: yarn A.
Rows 7–8: yarn B.
Rows 9–22: yarn A.
Rows 23–24: yarn B.
Rows 25–38: yarn A.
Rows 39–40: yarn B.
Rows 42–52: yarn A.
Rep 5 times more; total: 6 blocks.

Lace block
Using yarn B, work as pattern on page 70.
Rep 9 times more; total: ten blocks.
Using the position guide as reference, join each block to its neighbour through the loops on the reverse and below the top stitch loops in the last rnd.
The bottom edge of block 15 joins to the top edge of block 11.
The bottom edge of block 20 joins to the top edge of block 16.

FINISHING

Block the pieces using the ball band as a guide.
Lay out the pieces as shown in the position guide.
Join the knitted blocks using mattress stitch.
Attach the lace tubes to blocks 1 and 2 as shown.
Join the left-hand edge of block 7 to the top edge of block 1.
Join the right-hand edge of block 10 to the top edge of block 2.
Weave in and secure all the ends

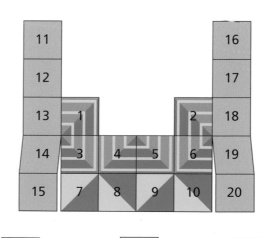

Three-stripe block

Two-tone block

Lace block

FILET THROW

The joy of filet crochet is that after the first row is established it is fairly stress-free. The yarns chosen are a mixture of fibres of a similar palette, with the softer yarns positioned towards the ends where they are most likely to be appreciated.

Finished size
100 x 150cm (40 x 60in)

Yarn
Rowan Classic Yarns, Cashcotton (35 per cent cotton, 25 per cent polymide, 18 per cent angora, 13 per cent viscose, 9 per cent cashmere; 130m [142yd]/ 50g [1¾oz]), #605 Magenta (A): 7 balls. Rowan Wool Cotton (50 per cent merino wool, 50 per cent cotton; 113m [123yd]/ 50g [1¾oz]), #959 Bilberry Fool (B): 4 balls; Rowan Pure Wool DK (100 per cent wool; 125m [136yd]/ 50g [1¾oz]), #042 Dahlia (C): 3 balls; #029 Pomegranate (D): 4 balls; Rowan Cotton Glace (100 per cent cotton; 115m [126yd]/ 50g [1¾oz]), #812 Ivy (E): 2 balls.

Equipment
4mm (USG-6) crochet hook
Tapestry needle

Abbreviations
Crochet
ch chain
om open mesh, ch 1, sk 1 sp or st, tr into the next st.
sm open mesh, tr into the next sp or st, tr into the next st.
tr treble crochet

Techniques
Filet crochet

Tension
Large flower block = 35 x 35cm (14 x 14in)
Small flower block = 15 x 15cm (6 x 6in)

BLOCKS

Large flower block
Foundation chain: using yarn A, ch 74.
Row 1: (as chart) yo, insert the hook into the 6th ch from the hook, work 1tr. This completes the first mesh. Cont to the end of the row using the chart as a reference and counting each ch as either a sp or a st. Read the chart from right to left on odd-numbered rows and left to right on even-numbered rows. Turn.
Row 2: ch 2 (counts as 1tr), cont to the end of the row, work the last tr into the 3rd ch of the beg-ch. Turn. Cont to foll the chart, ch 2 (counts as 1tr) at the beginning of each row, and work the last tr into the second ch of beg-ch before turning.
Fasten off yarn.
Rep 3 times more using yarn A.
Rep twice using yarn B.
Rep twice using yarn C.

Flower and filet block
Using yarn D, work as pattern on page 118.
Rep 5 times more; total: 6 blocks.

FLOWER

Using yarn D, work as pattern on page 116.
Rep 13 times more; total: 14 flowers.

Finishing
Block the pieces using the ball band as a guide.
Lay out the pieces as shown in the position guide.
Using yarn E, join the blocks using the treble crochet and chain seam on page 84, working the horizontal and then the vertical seams.
Surface crochet and bead one larger flower block in yarn C block as shown in the photograph. Join the flowers to the centre of both sides of the other larger flower blocks without embroidery. Using yarn B, edge the throw with a round of htr, then using yarn D, a round of reverse double crochet. Weave in and secure ends.

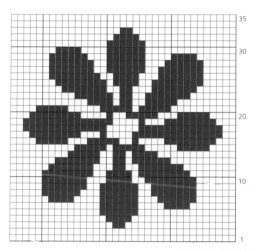

Finished size
30 x 10 x 25cm (12 x 4 x 10in)

Yarn
Rowan Cotton Rope (55% cotton, 45% acrylic; 58m [63yds]/ 50g[1¾oz]): #068 Harbour (A), 3 balls. Rowan Cotton Glace (100% cotton; 115m [126yds]/ 50g[1¾oz]): #827 Chalk (B), 2 balls; #817 Maritime (C), 2 balls; Rowan Handknit Cotton (100% cotton; 85m [93yds]/ 50g[1¾oz]): #335 Thunder (D), 1 ball. Rowan Kid Classic (70% lambswool, 26% kid mohair, 4% nylon; 140m [153yds]/ 50g[1¾oz]): #822 Glacier (E), 1 ball.

Equipment
4mm (US6) knitting needles
5.5mm (USI-9) crochet hook
4mm (USG-6) crochet hook
Tapestry needle

Notions
25mm (1in) D-rings, 2.
12mm (½in) suspender clips, 2.

Techniques
Surface crochet

Tension
11 stitches and 11 rows = 10 x 10cm (4 x 4in) in double crochet using a 5.5mm (USI-9) crochet hook and yarn A.
Not a tartan block = 15 x 15cm (6 x 6in)

Abbreviations
Crochet
blp back loop
bp back post
ch chain
dc double crochet
fp front post
tr treble crochet

Knit
k knit
p purl

BAG BASE

This is one of those pattern staples that you will use again and again; making it bigger, smaller, in one piece or in blocks. For the base, dark colours are definitely the best, and if the bag is to travel out and about a lot, choose a hardwearing fibre such as cotton.

Note: The bag base is rectangular with half-circle shaped sides at either end. A marker is placed in the first and last stitch of the straight edge, before and after the stitches that create the curve. After working the marked stitch, reposition the marker in the new stitch created into it.

BAG BASE

Foundation chain: using yarn A and 5.5mm (USI-9) crochet hook, ch 32.

Base

Rnd 1: insert the hook into the 3rd ch from the hook, work 1 dc, 1 dc into the blp of each ch until the last ch, pm in the last st worked, work 5dc into the next ch. Rotate the work, dc, into the flp to the st with a pm, work 1 dc into each of flp until the base of the beg-ch, pm in the last st worked, 5 dc into the next ch, join with a sl st to the beg-ch.

Rnd 2: ch 2, 1 dc into the blp until the marker, work 1 dc into the blp the next st, work 2 dc into the blps of each of the next 5 sts, 1 dc into the blp the next st, 1 dc into the blp each st until the marker, 1 dc into the blp the next st, work 2 dc into the blps each of the next 5 sts, join with a sl st to the beg-ch.

Rnd 3: ch 2, 1 dc into the blp of each st, join with a sl st to the beg-ch.

Rnd 4: ch 2, 1 dc into the blp of each st until the marker, work 1 dc into the blp the next st, work 1 dc into the blps next 3 sts, 2 dc into the blps of each of the next 4 sts, 1 dc into the blps next 3 sts 1 dc into the blp the next st, 1 dc into the blp of each st until the marker, work 1 dc into the blp the next st, work 1 dc into the blps next 3 sts, 2 dc into the blps of each of the next 4 sts, 1 dc into the blps next 3 sts, join with a sl st to the beg-ch.

Rnd 5: ch 2, 1 dc into the blp of each st, join with a sl st to the beg-ch.

Rnd 6: ch 2, 1 dc into the blp of each st until the marker, work 1 dc into the blp the next st, work 1 dc into the blps next 3 sts, 2 dc into the blps of each of the next 8 sts, 1 sc into the blps next 3 sts 1 dc into the blp the next st, 1 dc into the blp of each st until the marker, work 1 dc into the blp the next st, work 1 dc into the blps next 3 sts, 2 dc into the blps of each of the next 8 sts, 1 dc into the blps next 3 sts, join with a sl st to the beg-ch.

Rnd 7: ch 2, 1 dc into the blp of each st, discarding the markers after the sts have been worked, join with a

sl st to the beg-ch.
Turn.

Rnd 8: ch 3, 1 tr into the flp of each st, join with a sl st to the beg-ch.

Rnd 9: ch 3, 1tr into the blp of each st, join with a sl st to the beg-ch.

Rnd 10: 1 tr into the corresponding blp of the st at the base of row 8, *1 tr by inserting the hook through the next st and the corresponding blp of the st at the base of row 8, rep from * to the end of the rnd, join with a sl st to the beg-ch.

Sides

Rnd 11: ch 3 *tr fp around the post of the next st, tr bp around the post of the next st, rep from * to the end of the rnd, join with a sl st to the beg-ch.
Rep rnd 11 until the work measures 7.5cm (3in) from the base.
Fasten off yarn.

BLOCKS

Blocks 1 & 2

Using 4mm (US6) knitting needles, work as Not a tartan pattern on page 100.

Block 1: Substitute yarns: B for A; C for B; D for C; E for D.
Cast off.
Stitches of both yarns D and E are surface crocheted onto the swatch after the horizontal stripe pattern of yarns B and C has been completed.
Rep 3 times more.

Block 2: Work as for block 1.
Substitute yarns: C for A; B for B; E for C; D for D.
Rep 3 times more.

FINISHING

Block the pieces using the ball band as a guide.
Lay out the pieces as shown in the position guide with block 1 with the cast-on edge forming the right edge of the block and the reverse stocking stitch side of block 2 right side facing.
Using yarn C, join the blocks right side facing sides together using the single crochet and working the horizontal and then the vertical seams.
Using yarn C, attach the blocks to the bag base right side facing sides together using the double crochet through edge loops of the knitted blocks and the back loops of the bag base.

Using yarn D, edge the top edge with a round of htr, then, work a round of reverse double crochet.
Attach the suspender clips to the top edge centred over two adjacent blocks.
Double crochet two tabs for the suspender clips to attach to the front loops of the bag base, by using yarn D and inserting the hook into a loop of the corresponding base block to the suspender clasp, a distance of 3 sts for yarn D from the centre of the block. Ch 2, dc 5 times into bag st lps a st distance apart for yarn D. Work 5 rows of dc, fasten off yarn.

Handle

Foundation ring: using yarn A and 5.5mm (USI-9) crochet hook, ch 6 and join with a sl st to form a ring.

Rnd 1: Ch 4 (counts as 1 tr and 1 ch) *sk 1, 1 tr the next st, ch 1 st, rep from * once more, join with a sl st to the beg-ch.
Rep rnd 1 until the work measures 60cm (24in) from the foundation ring.
Fasten off yarn.
Attach each end to a D-ring using whip stitch.
Prise the D-ring open by moving the cut ends apart to the side, push through the bag fabric below the block seam on end of the bag enclosing as much fabric as possible. Slide the two ends of the D-ring back together and over sew to the inside of the seam.
Repeat with the other end of the handle.
Weave in and secure all the ends.

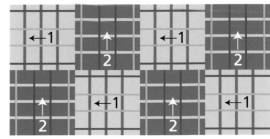

Arrows indicate direction of knitting

SYMBOLS AND ABBREVIATIONS

The symbols and abbreviations used follow a popular standard, but some may differ from what you have seen before, so it is always important to check the specific symbols used for each action in each publication or pattern.

KNITTING

Abbreviation	Instruction
ABCD	Yarn colours
alt	Alternate
beg	Beginning
cn	Cable needle
cont	Continue
dec	Decrease
dpn	Double-pointed needles
foll	Follow(ing)
k	Knit
k2tog	Knit two stitches together through the front of the loops
inc	Increase: as instructed in pattern
mb	Make bobble: as instructed in pattern.
patt	Pattern
pb	Place bead: as instructed in pattern.
p	Purl
p2tog	Purl two sts together
p2togtbl	Purl two sts together through the back of the loops
psso	Pass the slip stitch(es) over
rep	Repeat
rnd	Round
RS	Right side: the side of the work on display
skpo	Slip 1 stitch knitwise: k 1 stitch, pass the slipped stitch over
sl	Slip
st(s)	Stitch(es)
ssk	Slip 1 stitch knitwise: slip 1 stitch knitwise, insert the left-hand needle through the front of the two slipped sts and k together
tbl	Through the back of the loop
tog	Together
WS	Wrong side: the side of the work not seen
yb	Yarn back: take the yarn back between the needles from front to back of the work
yfwd	Yarn forward: take the yarn forward between the needles from back to front of the work
yo	Yarnover: yarn over needle to make a stitch

Symbol	Abbreviation	Instruction
*		Start of repeat
[ ]		Repeat the instruction within the brackets the stated number of times
□		K on the RS, p on the WS
▣		P on the RS, k on the WS
◨	ktbl	K through the back of the loop
▯		Sl st purlwise with yb
▭		Sl st purlwise with yfwd
☑	inc	Increase: k into the front and back of the same stitch on the RS, p into the front and back of the same stitch on the WS
▼	inc	Increase: p into the front and back of the same stitch on the RS, k into the front and back of the same stitch on the WS
▱		Ladder stitch: this symbol indicates the position of a stitch that is to be dropped to form a ladder. Work as stitch before it on the chart
⬇		Ladder stitch: drop the stitch off the needle without working it
⬆		Pick up a st from the edge
◼	mb	Make bobble: no turn bobble; [k into the front and back into the stitch] 6 times, pass the 2nd, 3rd, 4th and 5th sts on the right needle over the first and off the needle.
◉	pb	Place bead: yfwd on RS row slide a bead along the yarn to the base of the needle, sl the next st purlwise, yb; yb on WS row slide a bead along the yarn to the base of the needle, sl the next st purlwise, yfwd
⊞	pb	Place beads: slide the number of beads indicated along the yarn to the base of the needle between the sts indicated
✵	pb	Place bead: p on RS row, k on WS row, sliding a bead along the yarn to the base of the needle after each st
⋉		Short rows, wrap the stitch indicated: sl st purlwise, yfwd, sl st back to the left-hand needle, yb, turn work and proceed as instructed back along the next row charted

Symbol	Abbreviation	Instruction
⬚		Short rows, k wrapped stitch: lift the loop wrapped around the next stitch onto left needle and k the next two loops on the left-hand-needle tog or k the next two loops on the left-hand-needle tog through the back of the loops or as instructed in the patt
⬛		Grey box: no st or do not work st
◹	k2tog	Left-slanting dec using k
◺	ssk or skpo	Right-slanting dec using k
◹		Ssk with yarnover: yo, ssk
◹	p2tog	Left-slanting dec using p
◺	p2togtbl	Right-slanting dec using p
O	yo	Yarnover(s): yarn over needle to make a stitch
⭕		Yarnover with slipped st: yarnover, sl 1 st purlwise
●		Elongated stitch: k1, yo, drop the yo off the needle without working them on the foll row
⊘		Extended elongated stitch: insert the right-hand needle into the next st on the left-hand needle, wrap the yarn around the tip of the right hand needle the number of times stated into the symbol and complete the k st by drawing all the loops through the st on the left-hand needle. On the next row, work one of the loops and drop the rest off the needle.
If, the number of wraps is too large to draw through the st, work the number of wraps indicated before working the next k st as yarnovers and drop all the yarnovers on the next row
⬛	s2togk2psso	Double decrease: sl2 sts tog knitwise, k1, psso
⬛		I-cord bobble: [k3, sl sts back onto the left-hand needle] rep four times
◹	c2b	Cable two back: sl 1st onto cn and hold at the back of the work, k1, transfer the st from the cn back onto the left-hand needle, k1
Or without a cable needle: k into the front of the 2nd st on the left-hand needle and then k into the back of the first st, slipping both sts off the needle at the same time
◺	c2f	Cable two forwards: sl 1st onto cn and hold at the front of the work, k1, transfer the st from the cn back onto the left-hand needle, k1
Or without a cable needle: k into the back of the 2nd st on the left-hand needle and then k into the front of the first st, slipping both sts off the needle at the same time
◹	c2b	Cable 2 back: sl the next st onto the cn and hold at the back of the work, k1 from the left-hand needle, p1 from the cn
◺	c2f	Cable 2 forwards: sl the next st onto the cn and hold at the front of the work, p1 from the left-hand needle, k1 from the cn

Symbol	Abbreviation	Instruction
⬚	cr3f	Cross 3 forwards: sl the next 2 sts onto the cn and hold at the front of the work, k1 from the left-hand needle, sl the left st back onto the left-hand needle, p1, k1 from the cn
⬚	c4b	Cable four back: sl 2 sts onto a cn and hold at the back of the work, k2, transfer the sts from the cn back onto the left-hand needle, k2
⬚	c4f	Cable four forwards: sl 2 sts onto a cn and hold at the front of the work, k2, transfer the st from the cn back onto the left-hand needle, k2
⬚		Strand stitches: k2, yo, k1, pass the first k st worked in the sequence over the following k st, yo and last k st
⬚	t5b	Twist 5 back: sl 2 sts onto a cn and hold at the back of the work, k3, transfer the sts from the cn back onto the left-hand needle, p1, k1
⬚	t5b	Twist 5 back: sl 2 sts onto a cn and hold at the back of the work, k3, transfer the sts from the cn back onto the left-hand needle, k1, p1
⬚	t5f	Twist 5 forwards: sl 3 sts onto a cn and hold at the front of the work, k1, p1, transfer the sts from the cn back onto the left-hand needle, k3
⬚	t5f	Twist 5 forwards: sl 3 sts onto a cn and hold at the front of the work, p1, k1, transfer the sts from the cn back onto a to the left-hand needle, k3
⬚	t6b	Twist 6 back: sl 3 sts onto a cn and hold at the back of the work, k1, p2, transfer the sts from the cn back onto the left-hand needle, k2, p1
⬚	t6b	Twist 6 back lace: sl 3 sts onto the cn and hold at the back of the work, k1, k2tog, yo, transfer the sts from the cn back to the left-hand needle, k2, k2tog
⬚	t6b	Twist 6 back: k2, sl onto the cn and hold it at the front, sl 2sts onto a cn and hold at the back, k2 from the left-hand needle, p2 from the cn at the back, k2 from the cn at the front
⬚	t6f	Twist 6 forwards: sl 3 sts onto a cn and hold at the front of the work, p1, k2, transfer the sts from the cn back onto the left-hand needle, p2, k1
⬚	t8b	Twist 8 back rib: sl 4 sts onto a cn and hold at the back of the work, [p1, k1] twice, transfer the sts from the cn back onto the left-hand needle, [p1, k1] twice

USEFUL DEFINITIONS

Back of the work	The side facing away from you as you work
Front of the work	The side facing towards you as you work
Knitwise	Insert the needle as if to knit
Purlwise	Insert the needle as if to purl

CROCHET

Abbreviation	Instruction
ABCD	Yarn colours
alt	Alternate
bl	Back loop: yarn over hook as indicated by stitch, hook is inserted through the back loop only as it is presented at the point of working the st indicated
bp	Back post: yarn over hook as indicated by stitch, insert the hook from the back through to the front and back to the back, round the post of the st indicated and complete the st indicated
beg	Beginning
cont	Continue
foll	Follow(ing)
fl	Front loop: hook is inserted through the front loop only as it is presented at the point of working the stitch indicated
fp	Front post: yarn over hook as indicated by stitch, insert the hook from the front through to the back and back to the front round the post of the stitch indicated, and complete the stitch indicated
lp(s)	Loop(s)
mb	Make bobble: a group of stitches worked into the same space or st and worked to the point before the last yarn over hook to complete the stitches and joined with a yarn over hook loop drawn through all the stitches, as instructed in the pattern
patt	Pattern
pb	Place bead, as instructed in pattern
rep	Repeat
rev dc	Reverse double crochet (crab stitch): working from left to right, insert the hook into the st or space indicated, yarn over hook, pull loop
rnd	Round
RS	Right side: the side of the work on display
sk	Skip
sp	Space
st (s)	Stitches
WS	Wrong side: the side of the work not seen
yo	Yarn over hook

Symbol	Abbreviation	Instruction
*		Start of repeat
[ ]		Repeat the instruction within the brackets the stated number of times
▲		Starting point
←		Direction of working
△		Join in new yarn
▲		Fasten off yarn: cut yarn 10cm (4in) from the hook and draw the yarn through the loop
⌢	bl	Back loop: work the st indicated through the top, back, loop only of the st as presented at the point of working the st indicated
⌣	fl	Front loop: work the st indicated through the top, front, loop only of the st as presented at the point of working the st indicated
•	sl st	Slip stitch: insert the hook into the st or sp indicated, yo, pull lp through st and the lp on the hook
✿	sl stbl	Slip stitch through the back loop: insert the hook into the bl st indicated, yo, pull lp through st and the lp on the hook
○	ch	Chain: yo and draw through lp or slip knot on the hook
+ †	dc	Double crochet: insert the hook into the st or sp indicated, yo, pull lp through st, yo, draw lp through the 2 lps on the hook
⊼	dcbl	Double crochet through the back loop only (see bl above)
⊼	dcfl	Double crochet through the front loop only (see fl above)
⋏	2dctog	Double crochet together: work two single crochet sts into the sp or st indicated to the point of the final yo and the completion of the stitch, yo and draw the yarn through both sts to complete them
⊤	htr	Half treble crochet: yo, insert the hook into the st or sp indicated, yo, pull lp through st, yo, draw lp through all the lps on the hook
⊤	tr	Treble crochet: yo, insert the hook into the st or sp indicated, yo, pull loop through st, yo, draw lp through 2 lps on the hook, yo, draw yarn through the last 2 lps on the hook.
⊤	trbl	Treble crochet through the back loop only (see bl above)
⊤	trfl	Treble crochet through the front loop only: (see fl above)
⊤	trbp	Treble crochet round the back post (see bp left)
⊤	trfp	Treble crochet round the front post (see fp left)

Symbol	Abbreviation	Instruction
	trfpst	Treble crochet round the front post of the last st worked (see fp above)
	ttr	Triple treble crochet: yo 3 times, insert the hook into the st or sp indicated, yo, pull lp through st, then rep yo, draw lp through 2 lps on the hook until only 1 lp remains on the hook
	2trtog	Treble crochet together: work two double crochet sts into the sp or st indicated to the point of the final yo and the completion of the stitch, yo and draw the yarn through both sts to complete them
	dtr	Double treble crochet: yo twice, insert the hook into the st or sp indicated, yo, pull loop through st, then rep yo, draw lp through 2 lps on the hook until only 1 lp remains on the hook
	dtrbp	Double treble crochet round the back post (see bp above)
	dtrfp	Double treble crochet round the front post (see fp above)
	pb	Place bead: slide bead along yarn to the base of the hook or as indicated in patt
	pb	Place bead: slide bead along yarn to the base of the hook before the ch st indicated
	pb	Place bead: remove the hook and slide the bead along the yarn, insert the hook through the bead from the opposite side from the ch lp. Hook the ch lp and draw through the bead. Pass the bead onto the ch of sts before working the last yo
	cl	Cluster: a group of sts worked to the point before the last yo to complete the st and joined with a yo lp drawn through all the sts
	mcl	Make cluster: ch 2 st, 2tr sts in the sp below the base of the chain-2 and between the last 2 tr sts worked to the point of the final yo, yo draw yarn through all the lps on the hook
	ps	Puff or bobble stitch: a group of sts that meet at the top and the bottom; worked to the point before the last yo to complete the st and joined with a yo lp drawn through all the stitches. Note the appearance of the top of the group of stitches
	ml	Make loop: lp the yarn around the middle finger of the left hand, insert the hook into the st indicated, draw both strands of yarn at the base of the lp through the st, and complete the st indicated. Tighten the lp by pulling the two parts of the lp in opposite directions
	om	Open mesh in filet crochet: ch 1, sk 1 sp or tr st, tr into the next tr st or as indicated in patt

Symbol	Abbreviation	Instruction
	sm	Solid mesh in filet crochet: tr into the next sp or st, tr into the next tr st or as indicated in patt
		Add strand: fold an 20cm (8in) length of loose strand yarn B in half, insert the hook fp around the st indicated, draw the centre of the fold of yarn B through, ch the number of ch indicated the two strands of yarn B, using main colour yarn A yo, draw through last ch of yarn B and last st lp of yarn A. On following row this last ch is worked as a st. For the beaded version: slide a bead to the base of the hook after the ch indicated
		Broomstick crochet stitch: working from left to right, insert the hook into the st indicated, yo, draw the yarn through, and place the lp onto the knitting needle or strip of card
		Surface crochet: as indicated in patt

EQUIVALENT STITCH NAMES

The stitch names for some of the sts differ in the different areas of the world. Even more confusingly, the same names are used but they describe a different stitch. Check the list below and the descriptions above to make sure you know which stitch to work. The terms used in this book are compatible with the US and Continental Europe.

American	English
Single crochet	Double crochet
Half double crochet	Half treble crochet
Double crochet	Treble
Treble crochet	Double crochet
Double treble crochet	Triple treble crochet

USEFUL CONVERSION INFORMATION

We all have vintage yarns and needles or items that have come from another continent and it is always a useful exercise to convert unfamiliar terms and lengths to those you are familiar with and make a note of them for quick reference.

USEFUL CONVERSIONS

oz = g x 0.0352
g = oz x 28.35

yd = m x 0.9144
m = yd x 1.0936

in = cm x 2.54
cm = in x 0.3937

KNITTING NEEDLES

The old UK larger needle sizes were not standardized.

US size	Metric	Old UK and Canadian
0	2mm	14
1	2.25mm	13
—	2.5mm	—
2	2.75mm	12
—	3.00mm	11
3	3.25mm	10
4	3.5mm	—
5	3.75mm	9
6	4mm	8
7	4.5mm	7
8	5mm	6
9	5.5mm	5
10	6mm	4
10½	6.5mm	3
—	7mm	2
—	7.5mm	1
11	8mm	0
13	9mm	00
15	10mm	000
17	12.75mm	
19	15mm	
35	19mm	
50	25mm	

CROCHET HOOKS

The following sizes are plastic or aluminium crochet hooks, but not steel crochet hooks used for fine lace crochet. The old UK larger hook sizes were not standardized.

US size	Metric	Old UK
—	2.00mm	14
B-1	2.25mm	13
—	2.5mm	12
C-2	2.75mm	—
—	3.00mm	11
D-3	3.25mm	10
E-4	3.5mm	9
F-5	3.75mm	—
G-6	4mm	8
7	4.5mm	7
H-8	5mm	6
I-9	5.5mm	5
J-10	6mm	4
K-10½	6.5mm	3
—	7mm	2
L-11	8mm	0–1
M/N-13	9mm	00–000
N/P-15	10mm	
P/Q	15mm	
Q	16mm	
S	19mm	

YARN INFORMATION

The yarns used in the projects are perfect, but here is the essential information that will help with the substitution of the yarns and the creation of your perfection.

Apart from a few yarns, which have fibres that are not included within the Rowan Yarn range, Rowan Yarns or Jaeger Yarns have produced all the yarns in this book. The quality of the yarn is paramount to the success and longevity of a project and for me, the joy of good fibre is an essential part of my love for knit and crochet.

The project yarns have been listed below with the key pieces of information for yarn substitution, but remember to calculate the number of balls required by the number of yards and not by the yarn weight.

Rowan Calmer
CYCA #4, medium- or worsted-weight
80% cotton, 20% Elite polyester fibre
160m (175yd) per 50g (1¾oz) ball
Recommended tension: 21 sts and 30 rows to 10cm (4in)
with 5mm (US8) knitting needles

Rowan Classic Yarns, Cashcotton DK
CYCA #3, light- or DK-weight
35% cotton, 25% polymide, 18% angora, 13% viscose, 9% cashmere 130m (142yd) per 50g (1¾oz) ball
Recommended tension: 22 sts and 30 rows to 10cm (4in)
with 4mm (US6) knitting needles

Rowan Classic Yarns, Cotton Jeans
CYCA #4, medium- or worsted-weight
100% cotton
75m (82yd) per 50g (1¾oz) ball
Recommended tension: 19 sts and 26 rows to 10cm (4in) with 4.5mm (US7) knitting needles

Rowan Cotton Glace
CYCA #2, fine- or sport-weight
100% cotton
115m (126yd) per 50g (1¾oz) ball
Recommended tension: 23 sts and 32 rows to 10cm (4in) with 3.25–3.75mm (US3–5) knitting needles

Rowan Cotton Rope
CYCA #5, bulky- or chunky-weight
55% cotton, 45% acrylic
58m (63yd) per 50g (1¾oz) ball
Recommended tension: 15 sts and 20 rows to 10cm (4in) with 6mm (US10) knitting needles

Rowan Handknit Cotton
CYCA #4, medium- or worsted-weight
100% cotton
85m (93yd) per 50g (1¾oz) ball
Recommended tension: 19–20 sts and 28 rows to 10cm (4in) with 4–4.5mm (US6–7) knitting needles

Rowan Kid Classic
CYCA #4, medium- or worsted-weight
70% lambswool, 26% kid mohair, 4% nylon
140m (153yd) per 50g (1¾oz) ball
Recommended tension: 18–19 sts and 23–25 rows to 10cm (4in) with 5–5.5mm (US8–9) knitting needles

Rowan Pure Wool DK
CYCA #3, light- or DK-weight
100% wool
125m (136yd) per 50g (1¾oz) ball
Recommended tension: 22 sts and 30 rows to 10cm (4in) with 4mm (US6) knitting needles

Rowan Tapestry
CYCA #3, light- or DK-weight
70% wool, 30% soybean protein
120m (131yd) per 50g (1¾oz) ball
Recommended tension: 22 sts and 30 rows to 10cm (4in) with 4mm (US6) knitting needles

Rowan Wool Cotton
CYCA #3, light- or DK-weight
50% merino wool, 50% cotton
113m (123yd) per 50g (1¾oz) ball
Recommended tension: 22–24 sts and 30–32 rows to 10cm (4in) with 3.25–4mm (US3–6) knitting needles

INDEX

CREDITS

SUPPLIERS

Suppliers of Rowan Yarns

UK

Rowan Yarns
Green Lane Mill
Holmfirth
West Yorkshire
HD9 2DX
Tel: 01484 681881
www.knitrowan.com

US

Distributor:
Westminister Fibres Inc.
165 Ledge Street,
Nashua,
New Hampshire 03060
Tel: (603) 886 5041/5043

ACKNOWLEDGEMENTS

First I would like to thank Betty Barnden without whom there would be no section on embroidery and embellishment and who stepped into the breach when her skills and knowledge were sorely needed. Thank you.

All books have unsung heroes without whom they would not come to the printer's pass and I thank all of you. However, I can't leave unsung the talents and efforts of Liz Dalby and Julie Francis, as I look at the pages now, I don't know how we got this far but I know it was due to the talents and perseverance of these two people, thank you, it is appreciated.

The star of many a knitting and crochet book is the yarn and this book is no exception for which I would like to thank Rowan Yarns and Ann Hinchcliffe and Gemma Saxon for their advice.